PRAISE FOR
UNDER THE COVERS

"OMG I could not put this beautiful book down. Having a loved one who has mental health challenges, I appreciate Patricia's full expression of these challenges so that others can be drawn toward their own light."

SUSAN FREEMAN, MBA, PCC, executive coach, speaker, and author

"Authentic, gritty, sometimes whimsical. This is a bold telling of one woman's willingness to pay the price for fashioning a life she could call her own by drawing upon the strength and wisdom of her courageous forebears."

ANNETTE AUBREY, MSW, Reg. MSW, Systemic Family Constellations facilitator

"Whether you are a mental health professional, a reader looking for a compelling story, or a brave human being hoping to find companionship on a sometimes lonely road, *Under the Covers* will befriend, inform, and hypnotize you. Here is a feast of 'insider knowledge' about mental health interwoven with glimpses of a family's story and day-to-day life on the West Coast."

ARDEN HENLEY, Ed.D, RCC, vice president and principal of Canadian Programs, City University

---

"An unwavering response to life runs through this rich collection. At once poignant, sensuous, and entertaining."

SUSAN PAGE, executive director of San Miguel Writers' Conference and Literary Festival

---

"A gripping memoir of love and despair, Hetherington's *Under the Covers* reads like a ticking time bomb. So powerful is her prose that her recipe for lemon meringue pie had me on the edge of my chair. Here is an author riding roughshod over herself in the service of truth and self-discovery. I found myself speed-reading, as if the pages might self-destruct. What a ride! What a read!"

P.J. REECE, author of *Story Structure Expedition* and *Story Structure to Die For*

PATRICIA HETHERINGTON

UNDER

—THE—

COVERS

A LIFE *of* GUMPTION, PASSION,
GIFTS, *and* SECRETS

Patricia Hetherington

Rose Pointe
PUBLISHING

Rose Pointe Publishing
Gibsons, BC
www.patriciahetherington.ca

ISBN 978-0-9782795-1-6 (paperback)
ISBN 978-0-9782795-2-3 (ebook)

Produced by Page Two www.pagetwostrategies.com
Cover design by Naomi Macdougall
Author and cover photos by Ingeborg Suzanne (IS Photography)
Interior design by Taysia Louie
Printed and bound in Canada by Island Blue

18 19 20 21 22   5 4 3 2 1

To my sister Joann Hetherington

CONTENTS

"We have voices that want to be outspoken and bodies that want to move and shake, stories that need telling and secrets that need spilling."

GREGG LEVOY, *Vital Signs: The Nature and Nurture of Passion*

I

THE

CODE

———————

THE SOUND, SOFT as gossamer, rouses me from sleep. *Where did that come from?*

A familiar voice snipes in my head. *You know darned well where that comes from.* My inner critic flaunts her superiority. *And don't believe for a second that you can worm your way out of this one. Besides, how long has this thing hung around? Fifty years?*

You can call it a word—if you want to play semantics—but it's nothing more than a sound. Even so, it's stuck in your brain like an unwanted guest. Don't fool yourself—it's a force to be reckoned with. A living thing with a will of its own: an enfant terrible *demanding delivery and development.*

The acidic commentary winds up. *Let's face it, it's got you. Even if you have nothing but a silly sound to build a story around. If you ask my opinion, it's time to buckle down and start writing.*

I ADMIT IT: she has a point. Besides, I'm riled up now; there's no use belabouring the matter any longer. I climb out of bed, head to the long marble table I've used as my writing desk for years, pull out a chair, and plunk myself down. Tall brass candlesticks stand on the table like Hermes's columns, marking the threshold of a journey. My eyes travel past them to the lawn and ocean beyond— shimmering, rippled. A log floats by, set free from a boom or dragged from the shore by the fury of an undertow, the ocean claiming anything it wants as its own.

The moment presses down on me, forces my attention back to the work that awaits. Still, I stall; gaze at the sharpened HB pencils, run my hands reverently over the stack of paper, as if drawing assurance from its smooth white surface. My critic—vigilant as a hawk—sees me falter and stop.

Anxiety floods my body; my mind, like a bird on a wire, hops from one thought to another stored in the warehouse of my memory.

THE YEAR IS 1961. I'm with my mother in the sewing room of our new house in Smithers, British Columbia. I'm thirteen years old. A bulky wooden table dominates the cramped room; an old black piano sits along the far wall. Counting three other essential items—the ironing board, steam iron, and Singer sewing machine—there's barely enough space to turn around in. Sometimes my sister, Joann, is in the room playing the piano, but rarely sewing—not if she can help it.

I stand on the table, stretched to my full height, my head almost touching the ceiling. Still as stone and barely breathing, I compose myself for the supreme moment when my mother marks the hem of my skirt and my project is finished.

The two of us stuck in a tiny room, with me on the table and my mother about to perform the precise ceremony. She carries her wooden dressmaker's stick and walks solemnly around the table. Moving steadily clockwise, her eyes fixed on the unfinished hem of my skirt, she pauses at short intervals to squeeze a small, red rubber ball on the stick and discharge a fine, white line of chalk onto the fabric. *Pooooof!* she goes. *Pooooof! Pooooof!* The sound bewitches, captivates me for half a century, suggests magic and immediacy.

Pooooof! The genie pops out of the lamp. *Pooooof!* The prince appears. *Pooooof!* The royal carriage disappears at the stroke of midnight. *Pooooof!* Nothing more than a sound bite that has remained uncelebrated forever, and unfairly so. Until now.

Standing tall on the table, I feel proud that I have made the skirt myself, because it connects me to our family sewing tradition and to my maternal grandmother, Nan Capewell, who was a skilled seamstress.

NAN LIVED IN England in the early 1900s and worked at a manor house in the Sherwood Forest, sewing one-of-a-kind clothing for the two young daughters of a rich businessman whom she was required to call "Master." Ultimately, Nan grew weary of living cooped up like a bird in a cage. Reading her memoir, which she wrote decades later, it seems that she grew even more weary of being labelled an old maid.

At the age of thirty, Nan took matters into her own clever hands and immigrated to Canada, ending up alone in northern British Columbia, which, although harsh and isolated, offered her freedom to live her own life. She became the pioneer wife of a handsome French Canadian who was smart and hard working. He was a prospector who struck gold with his partners in the 1920s. He owned a livery stable, ran a pack train of horses, delivered goods and mail to remote settlements, and farmed a homestead near Telkwa.

Few women could have matched Joseph Bourgon, but Nan was equally determined and resourceful. At the centre of her being ran a swift-flowing current of energy that spilled over everything she created in the north country, untamed as it was.

Nan was a passionate gardener and avid homemaker who, unlike many pioneers, managed to feed her family on vegetables grown in her own garden and stock they raised themselves. Her flower beds flourished—producing armfuls of lilies, asters, snapdragons, sweet Williams, hollyhocks, brown-eyed Susans—enough to fill her home and satisfy her longing for beauty. She coddled her chicks as if they were her own precious children and kept her hens laying steadily to support a small egg business, keeping the money as her own independent source of income to spend on a rare treat. On a wood stove, Nan conjured up cream puffs made with fresh farm cream and angel food cakes made with the whites of one dozen eggs whipped to stiff perfection with a hand beater. On her Singer machine, she produced her own endless line of couture garments from any fabric she could find. She turned draperies into party dresses for her daughters and could take a man's woolen overcoat, turn it inside out, and transform it into something fetching and new. Occasionally her sister sent packages of dry goods and notions from Seattle, to help Nan keep herself and her beautiful daughters in fine clothes.

Nan was not only sought-after for her exceptional sewing but also loved for the hearty laugh that bubbled up through her stories. Friends and strangers alike drew strength from her robust spirit to endure the hardships of pioneer life. Such were her gifts—one of which I received.

As a young girl, I watched my grandmother intent at her sewing—bent over the machine, pumping the treadle, guiding the fabric under the needle, right hand turning the wheel in measured loops—in a world of her own, and I marvelled to see a garment gradually emerge from nothing more than fabric and an idea. I understood that before the cutting and pinning and sewing there was nothing—then suddenly there was something of beauty. When I was six years old I asked her to teach me to sew. She recognized my fascination with what I saw her doing and took my request seriously, never fussing that I could damage her prized possession. From those early days forward, we shared a mutual love.

The process amazed me and kept me happily tethered to a sewing machine throughout my high school years and into university, when I sewed up a storm during my holidays at home. Only hours before I boarded a plane to fly back to Simon Fraser University in Vancouver, I would hop into our car and drive over to visit Nan, who was living in an old folks' home by then. Despite her age she remained bright and feisty—and most definitely interested in my sewing.

One by one, I showed her the clothes I had made during my interlude at home, and we examined my work together. We looked briefly at the outside of a garment, which on one occasion was the jacket for a suit, but then quickly turned it inside out, to examine the less-touted but equally important side—to reveal the sewer's dedication and skill.

A surprise waited for Nan that day. In a brief shining moment, she caught sight of the jacket's pink acetate lining—so bold and unexpected she could only gasp and utter a sigh. The lining matched the pink angora sweater I planned to wear with the wool suit I was making, grey, with a pink fleck.

What a triumph! Nan in her late seventies and me at eighteen, sharing a moment of reckoning. We both knew that I had earned the sewing badge and joined the ranks of serious sewers in our family. Henceforth, I could be trusted to uphold the tradition of the family sewing code and the imperative of the four Fs: the love of fabric, fashion, fit, and flair.

Without ever talking about it, we both knew the serious sewers. They were the women who kept their machines set up, always ready to go, maybe even in a room of their own, as opposed to those who simply flirted with sewing, leaving their machines in their cases stowed on the floor of a closet.

THE VOICE OF my inner critic cuts through my musings. She picks at my thoughts. *What are you doing? Why are you fiddling around with this talk about pioneers and sewing?*

I'm getting ready to write, I reply.

Her scorn stings my ears. *Forget the nonsense! Drop the insouciance!*

Wait! I exclaim. *Words like that, words like* insouciance *are exactly what this is about. The love of words is what this "fiddling around" is about! I've been gathering steam, building energy with words and stories. We both know that writing must be coaxed to come forward—encouraged to show itself. Writing does not simply appear because we snap our fingers.*

I imagine her shaking her head and turning to leave, looking back over her shoulder and stating dismissively, *Whatever!* She wields her words like a pair of scissors and disappears.

NOTHING EXPLAINS THE power of the family sewing code better than the dozens of miniature photographs I find in old albums stashed at my home, many of which are still stuck to the black construction paper with glued-on triangle corners. But the love of sewing shines most brightly in the high style of several photographs and the captions noted below them.

"Sarah Toon—Nan's grandmother who taught her to sew—born 1823 Crimea."

"Sister Emily in white crepe de Chine blouse with lace trim—made by Nan, England 1905."

"Nan in Irish costume made for Hard Times Dance in Telkwa 1914. Admission 55 cents."

"Scottish Dance costumes made by Nan for concert 1928."

"The girls in their Sunday best and piqué hats 1935."

One photograph with a curious comment tops them all: a photograph of Nan Bourgon standing outside a chicken coop on a winter day, wearing rubber boots. The caption reads, "Nan 1939, black sateen dress with pots of chicken mash."

MY CRITIC BARGES back in and spits out the words. *What are you saying? Do you mean to say she was wearing a black sateen dress to do her chores?*

I try to mollify, then state the obvious. *Well, of course, what else do you do with a* good *dress that is no longer good, but still good enough for housework and chores? You wear it! Until it wears out. As simple as that, black sateen aside.*

WHEN NAN TURNED eighty, she traded in her sewing machine for a typewriter, taught herself to type, and embarked on a bold ambition to collect her stories and write a memoir. With the help of her daughters she published *Rubber Boots for Dancing* when she was ninety-four years old, to the acclaim of locals who understood only too well that without Nan the old stories would have scattered in the north wind, with the pioneer voices silenced forever. Nan died at ninety-five, signing off in her own words: "Life was difficult, but it was a good life."

FIVE DECADES HAVE disappeared since the day in the sewing room with my mother. The years close around the stories. Nan's stories were picked and preserved in her memoir, like jars of jam lining the shelf of a pioneer larder. And mine, I relive less from memory and more from a somatic sense.

Today, half a century later, I sit at the marble table and look out to the ocean. The tide pulls the water sideways like a sheet of light; a yellow-throated hummingbird appears at the window, a harbinger from the other side. Hermes watches—protective, attentive. My critic stops nattering and my mind settles; the anxiety abates.

New sensations stir inside me. My spirit quickens; my heart leaps. *It's coming! It's coming!* The precious *enfant* claims its deliverance and arrives with a swoosh. I grab a pencil, select a sheet of paper, and press down hard—one onto the other—and just like that, I start writing!

Pooooof! Pooooof! Just like that. *Pooooof!* I start writing.

2

THE

DART

———————

THE DART RUNS deep in my family sewing tradition. Like the Bulkley River in northern British Columbia, which runs swift and cold and teeming with trout, the dart is also treacherous. Calling it treacherous may be overstatement, but the dart cuts both ways. Often helpful and beautiful, it also has a shadow side, particularly as it relates to the dictates of fabric, fashion, fit, and flair—the four Fs of the family sewing code. The danger of the dart is its demand for fit, which drives a strong imperative in one's psyche. But before plunging into these swift-moving waters, there is the question: *What is a dart?*

A dart is a sewing technique used to shape a garment to the body and, specifically, accentuate the bust, hips, and waist. Most importantly, the dart functions in service to the fit.

MRS. PEARSON, MY high school sewing teacher, holds the keys to the kingdom. I see her still: a long lanky woman waving her large dressmaker scissors, demonstrating the procedure with needle, thread, and fabric, while offering a fluid stream of instructions. "First you turn your garment inside out, grab the excess fabric, fold it into a straight line, thumb-press along the folded edge, slide the thing under your presser foot, and sew a straight line down the fabric, beginning wide at the top and narrowing to a point at the bottom.

"Finally, you turn the garment right side out and press flat. There you have it—your dart—and we can continue."

DARTS HAVE COME a long way in my life. I've used them in ways I never imagined as a girl in school, sewing blouses and skirts in Smithers. Most of my ventures have been useful and satisfying; others I do not care to repeat. But there's no doubt about it: darts pack power—working for the greater good of alterations—and often delivering surprisingly effective results. Because of this intimate connection, the words *dart* and *alteration* can be used almost interchangeably, and I attest to applying these ideas successfully in a variety of ways, including

1 sewing delicate darts on the fine lace cups of a camisole;

2 adding hefty darts on the four corners of a new fitted sheet—making it conform to the promise of "fitted";

3 taking in numerous pants and capris at the waist, sewing the dart *through* the waistband, which could be considered a travesty of the family code;

4   nipping in a badly shaped but gorgeous white cotton
    blouse by running double darts down the front and
    back of the garment; and

5   altering a pair of fleecy pyjamas—although on princi-
    ple I do not believe in altering pyjamas, nor do I care
    much for wearing them.

However, some alterations I simply refuse to repeat,
namely

1   jeans of any sort that mangle my thread and break my
    machine needles; and

2   sheets of any sort: flat or fitted, although I have been
    gravely tempted to add a length of cotton on to the bot-
    tom of a new flat sheet—to prevent it from pulling out
    and leaving my feet exposed and cold, and generally
    creating a sloppy appearance.

Still, I confess that I recently altered the same flat sheet
I refused to touch. But what could I do? I found the perfect piece of white fabric cut from a duvet cover I had
shortened years ago. But I excuse the lapse—in service
to the four Fs of the family code. The situation becomes
painfully clear. The impulse to dart and alter is deeply
ingrained in my family and covers a wide swath of life.

BY SPRING 2010, half a century after the sewing classes,
I had ventured far from Smithers. I embarked on a trek
across northern Spain that not only beat up my body and
spirit, but also dismantled the basic tenets of my life as
governed by the family code. With a hardy man as my

companion, I rose to the challenge of walking the ancient pilgrimage route called El Camino de Santiago, or St. James's Way. Mid-point on the five-hundred-mile route, I called it madness. Each morning I awakened in the dark; heaved myself down a set of rickety bunks—often from the top of three beds teetering together; pulled on dank clothes; packed my belongings in the tiny beam of a headlamp; and groped my way past rows of snoring pilgrims, careful not to rob them of the luxury of a longer sleep. I found my way through ancient doors of a *refugio* and stepped into another bracing day, hauling a sixteen-pound purple pack that held only the barest essentials for a month-long journey. I reassessed the value of each article constantly by considering its weight as much as its function. With the exception of a few things—a change of clothes, soap, and a microfibre towel; a pen, paper, and passport; euros and a bank card; rain gear, headlamp, and a sleeping bag—little survived the culling. Neither an extra pair of woollen socks nor a miniscule pair of pink earplugs.

One morning I awakened at five o'clock. The buzz in the crowded bunkroom where dozens of weary pilgrims had slept was that it had snowed during the night. Incredulous, I shook my head. *Snow in Spain, in April?* But snow it was and there was no use snivelling. Unfortunately, my hasty actions the week before left me in an awkward bind I could have avoided. Relying on the improving weather we had enjoyed over the previous few days, and acting on impulse, I had packed my warmer, heavier clothes and sent them home. Granted, this lightened my load but limited my options. Fantasizing that I could stay behind in the *refugio* for a day or two to wait out the snow was futile. Our hosts, mainly older, wiser, no-longer-walking-the-Camino men and women, had other ideas, including the requirement that all pilgrims be up and out by eight o'clock—regardless of snow, a sprain, or a nasty case of the flu. It was non-negotiable. A rule of the road.

What could I do? The familiar pressure to dress, pack, and get on the road left little time for creative thinking, but my instinct for survival kicked in with a clever idea. I grabbed my already-packed bag, thrust my arm deep inside, and hauled out my sleeping bag.

Yup, that's what I'll do! I decided. *I'll wear my sleeping bag—unzipped and wrapped around my body.*

But wait! How will I hold it up? Keep it closed? Meanwhile, I caught the attention of a friendly Australian woman standing in the aisle between our bunks.

As I wrapped myself in the opened bag and tried walking in my new gear, she moved toward me and produced a huge safety pin from her own pack. She stood there, holding it out to me with a girlish grin plastered on her face. I grabbed the pin like a hungry waif and plunged it into the slippery nylon padding; my strange garment held secure around my neck with a single pin. Within minutes I headed out into the snowy morning with the long green garment floating down and around my body, feeling deeply satisfied with my innovation. Occasionally the poufy fabric flopping around my ankles impeded my walking, but I was content to settle for covered and warm.

For three days I walked in the bag, during which time the safety pin took a beating from my opening, closing, and forcing it through the resistant nylon. But I took no chances and tended it carefully, religiously shaping and straightening it to keep it in good working order. My health and perhaps my sanity depended upon it.

On the third day out, my walking companion and I stopped mid-morning at a desolate café seeking, as always, the warmth of hospitality and the chemical hit of espresso. To our delight, we found our friend and fellow pilgrim David, a handsome young German, leaning against the bar.

"Patricia," he announced warmly, rushing over to give me a hug before stepping back and regarding me intently. "You're a chrysalis!"

David nailed it. Of course I was a chrysalis, with my caterpillar head poking out of the shiny green cocoon. But the analogy was even more complete. Like the caterpillar whose body disintegrates within its protective covering, I was unaware that my body and psyche were undergoing mutations as well.

There are strange things done in the midnight sun. There were strange things done on the way to Santiago, triggered when I was forced to give up my expectation of looking good and relinquish the demand for fashion and fit in everything I wore. We crossed the terrain and marked the miles the only way we knew how: taking two steps at a time—typically walking for eight or nine hours each day—my mind often dazed, my spirit often worn thin and weeping. Still I remembered why I walked the Camino.

I walked the Camino to leave behind a habituated way of appearing in the world; stretch my body to the screaming point and send my overactive brain on sabbatical; reject agendas and accountability; cast off technology and rely on my senses; dull the din of the world as fomented by headlines and news; test my mettle; and hear sacred music in churches and monasteries.

WITH SANTIAGO BECKONING on the horizon and the promise of benediction mere hours away at a pilgrims' mass in St. James's cathedral, I stumbled more than I walked; moved more by will than by strength. Once inside the cathedral and still wearing my pack like a purple appendage, I fell to my knees on a hard, unforgiving kneeler, made the sign of the cross as I bowed my head, and waited for thoughts to form, prayers to pray. None came. Instead my emotions told a story of exhaustion, gratitude, awe, and elation. I marvelled at the scope and grandeur of the baroque cathedral: the blazing candles, brilliant chandeliers, and gilded statues; the silver casket believed to hold the remains of St. James; Catholic priests pulling the massive metal censer up and into the heavens on a rope thick as a wrist, with the censer swaying overhead and, like a burning orb, spilling frankincense into the cathedral. I recognized that I belonged to this throng of pilgrims from around the globe and throughout the centuries, who likewise had responded to the call of the Camino.

LOOKING BACK AT my journey and in particular at the days I spent as a chrysalis draped in the soft green shroud,

I recognize what a therapist might describe as an "initiation"—a process leaving its mark on my psyche as well as a force rendering my body.

When I return home, my body is unrecognizable and foreign. It has been almost a month since I have had a good look at myself in a mirror. In the absence of a constant image reporting back to me how I look, I have missed seeing what I feared most. I have become "reedy"—the precise word a fellow writer and pilgrim uses to describe his own body after walking the Camino. I groan with shock and dismay. Reedy—with its suggestions of scrawny, sinewy, gaunt.

I plunge into confusion and shame, trying to avoid what my mirror is telling me. But local folks are quick to set the record straight. "My God, Patricia, you're so thin. Did you mean to lose that much weight? You can't afford to lose weight. I thought you'd come home full of energy!"

My body is now common property—open to others' interpretations and judgments. I struggle while attempting to remain invisible, inhabiting a strange liminal space, slipping along the sidelines of my life, neither *here* nor *there*, neither *this* nor *that*. My closet holds only horror, offers up only sloppy-fitting clothes. I resort to wearing a couple of outfits and ignore the rest—unable to confront the reality of what has happened to my body and hating the clothes that represent this drastic change.

Fall, with its inclement weather and need for warmer clothes, brings an onslaught of panic. *How do I dress this body? Is it still "shape-shifting" or is this "it"? What, if anything, do I buy?* Still stuck in the muck of the chrysalis, I have no way of knowing. One evening in late September, my sister Joann rifles through my closet, hauling out garment after garment, trying to find clothes that will still fit me.

She grabs a pair of black stretch jeans. "What about these?" she asks. "What the heck," she continues, "they're brand new!"

"And too big by a mile," I counter.

The jeans were sexy when they fit, but now they simply look ridiculous. By this time, Joann has gathered a full head of steam and is not about to stop. She spits out the words, "Just take them in with some darts!"

I could retort in a snooty way, "Any real sewer knows that there's only so much a dart can do," but I don't. Besides, I have tried this manoeuvre before and know from experience that taking in this much fabric from a waistband—particularly with heavy denim—is a recipe for disaster. With the darts sewed *through* the waistband, the back pockets inevitably stick out and float away from the jeans, making the solution no solution at all.

But I do the darts anyway, out of desperation. Mrs. Pearson's voice echoes in my head as I follow her instructions:

1   grab the excess fabric at the waistband;

2   pin and baste the darts; and

3   stuff the jeans under the presser foot of the machine and sew—wide at the top and narrowed to a point.

I attempt to iron the darts flat, but the eight layers of denim resist my efforts. The result is awkward and uncomfortable. The darts—nasty little creatures that they are—dig into my waist, into my kidneys. I hate the jeans—more than before—and banish them, once again, to the back of my closet. I also hate this whole messy process I find myself in and take no comfort in the caterpillar's story of transformation.

One and a half years have passed since my initiation in the green cocoon. With some assurance, I can finally say, *This is me. This is my body. It is safe to settle in and take up residency again*. But, unknown to me, the jeans have taken on a life of their own, rising up and returning like a fabric spectre. Unbidden thoughts come to mind as I wake one morning with a sudden inspiration. I leap out of bed and follow the impulse:

1   find the jeans;

2   slice the stitches of the dart with my thread picker;

3   remove the loose threads; and

4   baste along the impressions made by the dart with a contrasting thread to mark the original outlines.

At this stage in the process I stand at a precipice, dangerously close to violating the family code and committing a cardinal sin of sewing. I pause to consider the consequences and at the same time imagine my sewing teacher, Mrs. Pearson, discovering what I am thinking.

She jumps toward me, flapping her hands as if to say, *No! No! No!* Oblivious to her pleas, I pick up my scissors and hear her squeal. *Cut out the darts? That will unleash all manner of turmoil!* But my course is set. I leap over the edge, dealing with one dart at a time:

1 grip my scissors;

2 nudge up to the basting thread;

3 cut down one side and up the other;

4 pull the fabric dart away from the garment and toss it aside;

5 proceed to the sewing machine;

6 overcast the raw edges to prevent fraying;

7 find an iron-on denim patch;

8 cut a strip approximately one inch wide and the length of the cut edges;

9 place the iron-on patch behind the edges—glue side up and facing the inside of the jeans;

10 snuggle the two sides together; and

11 iron the patch firmly into place, pressing both sides of the jeans.

I repeat the same procedure with the second dart and I'm done. The jeans are a triumph! Smooth to a fault and couture-comfortable. Further to my delight, I realize that I have reached a level of innovation with my daring dart manoeuvre rarely, if ever, found in the annals of sewing.

When I wear my jeans these days, I feel a quiet thrill run through my body, for I have freed myself from the dictates of the dart—as my mother and generations before her watch the goings-on from their celestial home. My hunch is that my mother is having a fit, but my grand-mother, Nan, is loving the flair.

3

THE

BUN

ARLY INTO A reckless month in Maui, 1970, one
morning before dawn, driving an ice-slick road from
the lookout at the rim of Haleakala Crater we hit
black ice. My sister, Joann, screams as she spins the wheel
of our Rent-A-Wreck, her hands white-knuckled as she
struggles to keep the car on the road. With no guardrail
in sight, with the brakes bad and the tires worse, the car
sails across the surface, bounces over the edge, and begins
rolling down a treacherous slope covered with volcanic
boulders. One lone pine with branches outstretched like
arms of a guardian blocks our way. The car slams to a
stop against the tree, as if by intervention from Pele herself—the Hawaiian goddess of volcanoes and fire—who
saves our skin that morning.

But the close call does nothing to prevent us from
enjoying the company of a curious assortment of men
throughout the month, including Kris Kristofferson, who

travels with us in the blue rental car, seducing us with songs that we play on the cassette machine throughout our stay on the island. We form a quick bond with Kris, embracing his philosophy of life that suits our new-found freedom, what with Joann now one year into her career in retail merchandising, and me at twenty-two and just out of university with a degree in education and my English and French majors.

One song receives the most airtime. In a duet called "I'd Rather Be Sorry," Kristofferson pulls no punches in stating his case.

I'd rather be sorry for something I've done
Than for something that I didn't do.

HE'S GOT MY number and I need no convincing. Furthermore, in my French studies when I first hear Edith Piaf sing, *Non, je ne regrette rien,* I recognize my sort of woman. But between the two of them, Kris a no-guts-no-glory guy endowed with a gift for gritty lyrics, and Edith a tiny woman with a warbly voice, it's all the same. Whether it's "I'd rather be sorry" or "no regret," neither has the slightest regard for life's vicissitudes. I align easily with their thinking.

Besides, our mother, Antoinette Emily Bourgon, has been planting seeds of these ideas for years, as Joann and I were growing up in Smithers, British Columbia. Ultimately, whatever their words, Kristofferson and Piaf are singing the same song, which tells me that living a life of no regret demands a boldness that most people deem too risky. This attitude allows no tolerance for half measures. No partly bold, no half-committed, no half-hearted. Or, in our mother's words, no half-assed that inevitably leads to regret later in life, when we begin to take stock in earnest. Admit our mistakes, acknowledge those we have injured, and make amends *when* and *where* we are still able. Often it is too late. Almost without warning, we find ourselves in *torschlusspanik*: gate-closing panic, locked outside the warmth of hearth and home like Heathcliff standing on a howling moor, powerless to change circumstance or undo wrong.

It seems the best insurance is acting with conviction in the present before the will to make outrageous moves begins to wane. Our mother, either by virtue of an authority vested upon her by the Catholic Church, or by virtue of being president of the Catholic Women's League, likes to remind us, "The sin of omission is more egregious than the sin of commission." In Catholic terms, this means that omission is a cardinal sin, whereas commission could be considered venial. Occasionally she elaborates on the theme with a slightly different sentiment: The road to hell is paved with good intentions.

With our mother and her reputation as a doer and a thinker, there is no argument. She is a teacher and a smart one at that. In her mind there is no fudging the simple truth: omission is omission. By the time I stand poised to step into the world, I have fallen in line and accepted her no-regret philosophy as a guiding principle. But it is not until my thirties, when I have tested my wings enough and tasted enough success, that the philosophy starts to muscle in—when the stakes are huge. Two stories deserve attention: one, a business story, the other a love story. Both unfold when there is nothing left to lose.

THE FIRST STORY takes place in downtown Calgary, 1980, when the city is an epicentre of international industry. Oil and gas companies explode with unprecedented growth; construction companies struggle to satisfy the demand for prime office space. In the height of this real estate frenzy I am the leasing agent for a fifteen-story building that, while still under construction, has an accepted offer for the entire project, subject to board approval. Late in the day of the board meeting the deal crashes. The board's assessment? Wrong location. The building is back on the market.

The world becomes silent and falls away.

I drop into a stillness within that is not unlike the space I encounter as I prepare one starry night to walk on hot coals with a group of spiritual seekers on a ranch outside Calgary. When I step onto the bed of glowing embers, I hear the crunch of coals beneath my feet but experience no pain. Neither fear nor thought exists. Instead, a certainty born of clear intention and an unencumbered heart compels me to walk safely along the seething bed. Once again Pele protects me from injury.

Insight, like a flash of metal in an ancient forge, shows me what to do. *Carpe diem.* Seize the day. I grab the phone book and dial the number for the president of Canada's largest private oil company, who I know is looking for office space similar to the size of my building. Seconds later he picks up his home phone and identifies himself. I catch my breath and dive in, stating my name and company and the reason for my call, and ending by asking if he will see me. Businesslike yet gracious, he invites me to his house at seven o'clock in the evening.

I arrive punctual and impeccably dressed in a designer suit and French pumps. His wife greets me at the door and ushers me into his office. Our time together is brief but sufficient for me to inform him that there is a building back on the market and available for lease. He listens carefully as I outline the benefits of my project, matching what I believe is important to him with features I can offer. When I finish, he pauses before speaking, and only then to tell me that he is still committed to another building that he has been negotiating on. Our business concludes. We stand, say thank you, and shake hands; he walks me to the door, opens and closes it behind me. I drag appreciative breaths into my lungs as I step into the brisk air.

Do I feel like a fool?

No!

I feel lighthearted and proud that I have seized the day, certain that if I had not done what I needed to do, my regret would be less about the loss of a large commission than the loss of courage. It was omission I would have regretted, and rightly so. As Antoinette Emily's daughter, and imprinted as I am by her forceful ideas, I really have no choice. The following morning I send the president's wife a box of cut flowers and a card thanking them for their hospitality.

THE LOVE STORY also takes place in Calgary, five years after the business story. For ten days every July since 1912, the city transforms into the Wild West, with men and women alike swept into one long unbridled party. Few are immune to Stampede fever brought on by dancing until dawn, booze at breakfast, ladies with come-hither smiles wearing tight jeans and flashy jewellery, and guys with swagger wearing Levis, skinny ties, and plaid shirts with pearl buttons—everyone and everything inciting the town into a hotbed of music, touch-dancing, promise, and impulse.

Sonja, my childhood friend from Smithers at her first Stampede party, straddles the heaving mass of a mechanical bull that snorts and humps like a flesh-and-blood beast. One hand grips the saddle horn, the other waves at the crowd gathered around her. A grin plastered on her face, she hollers for the hell of it. The beast winds down and lurches to a stop. Sonja, sated, slides off the creature. The next rider mounts the bull to loud, lewd comments. Sonja grabs my arm, revelling in the Stampede spirit and a weekend away from her two kids left at home with a babysitter. We swing toward the wooden platform set up outside for dancing. Best friends, thirty-seven years old, out for the night: Sonja divorced, me unmarried, both eager to make the best of the party. Out of the crowd a stranger with a black hat strides toward me, his eyes fixed and appraising as he approaches. "Patricia!" he declares like he's known me for years. "My friend John has pointed you out before." Without warning—maybe sick with Stampede fever—he grabs me in his arms and kisses me, then remembers to introduce himself.

"Brian," he says simply. "Would you like to dance?"

"Yes," I reply.

We dance until the band shuts down, saving the last dance for each other before driving to my home. The following morning I know that he's my man. Some time later, when he tells me that he's involved with another woman from the United States whom he met shortly before meeting me, like Lady Macbeth, it never occurs to me to pull out. And while I might consider myself forewarned, the knowledge of the triangle does nothing to soften the blow of heartache. Ultimately, I resolve to accept the pain as part of the deal—for the possibility of marrying him. The arrangement continues for nine anguished months as he returns to Calgary and leaves again to be with her.

Once, he arrives at my home after a longer-than-usual time away and tells me that he is marrying the American woman. The news—equally an emotional and physical blow—dumbfounds me. I tumble into oblivion where I remain for three days, too stunned to think, to move, to function. *Not that I don't know of her existence—but this? Marry her? Impossible.* Occasionally I want to gag but nothing comes up. Wrung out, wrecked, I stop resisting when—without warning—the fog in my mind clears. I know what to do. Carpe diem.

I need to write the story of our relationship to make it real. For me, to understand the often-terrible some-times-ecstatic relationship, and for him, to know the part he plays in fostering an emotional awakening in me, for which I have no words. Like no other man, he cuts through the cool exterior I show the world, to reveal a woman longing for more intimacy and meaning. He extends a silken cord to make it safe to descend into the labyrinth within me in search of a more authentic self. The writing, fuelled by adrenalin and urgency, consumes my attention, wiggles its way into my thoughts, snatches every image and memory lodged in my heart, claims any moment as its own, and bores relentlessly into the night. The heat of the process softens the story to flow unhin-dered onto the reams of old-style punched computer paper I use for writing, and the story grows long like Rapunzel's hair. In less than a month I produce a rough draft: written, transcribed, printed, and packaged for a courier to deliver to his American office.

Do I feel like a fool?

No!

I feel calm and satisfied that I trusted a curious impulse to give voice to my story, in an attempt to excise every part of him from the cells of my body and move on with my life. Once again, devastating news propels me to action.

Five weeks pass with no response, until one day when he returns to Calgary and calls to ask if he can see me. We meet later that day, sitting outside in his car next to the building where I have attended a workshop. He makes no mention of the couriered package but wastes no time in telling me that he is *not marrying* the American woman. Instead he asks *me* to marry him.

I seize the moment before he finishes and respond with a single word, "Yes!" We marry two months later—both of us convinced that if I had not plunged in and sent him my story he would have continued on his path to the altar with another woman. I would have missed the whole thing: love, marriage, and the baby carriage. I would have missed the biggest deal of my life and the regret would never end.

THERE IS NO doubt. Life with its delights and disasters is fraught with possibility for regret. Big or small, transformative or inconsequential, each story packs power enough to raise havoc, fester over time, and linger long past a reasonable expiry date. The dazzling deals of boardrooms and bedrooms speak for themselves, but the smaller deals of life are not to be forgotten.

From an early age I fall under the thrall of my Aunt Janet's heavenly cinnamon buns, which she serves from her kitchen in Smithers at special family gatherings: Christmas, New Year's, and the occasional birthday. From eating these treats year after year, I learn to expect that some things will remain constant over time and produce the same pleasures: the same size and soft texture, the sticky caramelized topping, the delicate dough studded with raisins, the slim spool of bun at the centre—not unlike the oyster tucked along the backbone of a chicken or turkey, likewise delightful and delicious. Except for a surprisingly few specimens I encounter elsewhere in my life, decades later my aunt's buns remain unrivalled, steadfast reminders of the goodness in life.

When I leave home at seventeen, I abandon all thought of buns. My mind fixes on more compelling matters until I am in my mid-forties and living on the Sunshine Coast of British Columbia with my husband, Brian, and three-year-old daughter, Sarah. Shortly after our arrival in 1991, I hear news of a bakery that serves a prize-worthy cinnamon bun, located in Lund, British Columbia, at the last stop on Highway 101, ninety-five miles up the coast from where we live and nine thousand miles from the beginning of the highway in Quellón, Chile. The tiny town of Lund boasts two claims to fame: its unique location at "The End of the Road," as proclaimed on a banner strung high over Main Street; and Nancy's Bakery, found at the end of the dock, at the end of the road. In this sense Lund is a big deal.

Is the cinnamon bun our only reason for driving up and down the highway, incurring the cost of food, gas, and overnight lodging in the historic Lund Hotel? The answer is *probably*. I call it "reconnaissance," because we are hunting a rare species. Decades after we first taste Nancy's buns, I do not remember their precise qualities, but I remember they don't disappoint, ranking up there with my aunt's buns. Nancy and Lund live up to their enviable reputations and I take solace in the fact. All is well with the world. As we depart town and drive beneath the banner calling out after us, "See You Soon!" there is poignancy in our leave-taking as we wave goodbye to no one in particular.

We return to Lund eight years later, like pilgrims returning to Lourdes seeking the healing waters. In a similar way we are seeking the sweet succor of Nancy's buns. As we drive into town it becomes painfully clear. Something is wrong. The proud banner proclaiming "The End of the Road" is missing. So, too, is Nancy's Bakery, previously perched at the end of the dock. We smell subterfuge. Minutes later a woman points us in the right direction and we discover Nancy's a short walk away, now a slick new café in an impressive West Coast building with cedar beams, rock, and slate floors, and massive windows overlooking an outdoor seating area planted with indigenous grasses. Without question this newness is stunning, but for me the changes feel disconcerting. In an attempt to counter my disappointment over what ensued after we found the bakery, I fire off an email to a friend who will grasp my true feelings. The subject says it all, but the loss requires further explanation.

Subject: Nancy has changed her bun!

OMG—all the way to the end of the road—to find that Nancy has changed her bun. Her staff knows nothing of the matter but the issue is suspiciously clear. The new bun is not the right size or texture, not the rich caramelized version, and without the slim spool at the centre. This is a drastically different specimen. The new bun looks

curiously like a Costco knockoff, suffocating in Saran
Wrap. My world is in shambles. To show their solidar-
ity, Brian and Sarah have abstained as well. To partake
is inconceivable. Still, I swallow my dismay and turn my
thoughts to being on the road again, in pursuit of other
worthy specimens. The bun has changed, but I carry on.
Love P.

The next morning before heading home we stop at the
fancy new café for a quick breakfast, when the puzzle of
the missing banner is solved. Perhaps the change occurs
while the town dozes through successively uneventful
years, assured that its remote location confers upon it
a uniqueness that will endure. But this is not to be; the
evidence is in front of our faces. A massive blackboard
nailed to a wall decrees shamelessly, "The Lund of the
Rising Bun." The town's pride of place—usurped by
Nancy's prize confection! And here it is—painted on the
board in brazen colours, a self-important, oversized sun-
bun rising in the east, hovering over the sleepy town like
a benevolent potentate. The town now plays second fiddle
to one of its own. Suddenly, this is all too much: a surfeit
of emotion and not enough sweetness. It is time to leave.

Years lapse before we give the matter of buns another
thought. But when we do, it is serendipitous the way
Sarah and I are wandering along a sidewalk across from
the Intrawest Hotel in Whistler, after a day of skiing on
Blackcomb Mountain. Leisurely minding our business,
peering into store windows, buns are the last thing on
our minds, when suddenly we spy in the display case of a

bistro a batch of glorious golden cinnamon buns. Standing outside the frosted window of Ciao Thyme, we declare them top quality on the spot. Even before we devour our buns, we name them "The Tried and True." The way they appear is remarkable—how they offer themselves up for our pleasure without drama or disappointment. The whole experience restores my faith in the constancy of life. All is well with the world.

MY NEXT ROAD trip of significance is in 2012, when I am driving the triangle tour in Mexico between Todos Santos, El Triunfo, and La Paz with my writing companion, Eda. Of the three towns, El Triunfo is the highlight of our trip, and although no longer the booming mining town it once was in the 1860s, we discover gold there nonetheless. At first, we see nothing to recommend the town; it looks lifeless and dry, shrivelled like tumbleweed. A feeling of ruin hangs about the place. Our plan is to gas up and hit the road as fast as we can. But as we finish at the pump, a bright-eyed Mexican boy rushes over to our Hertz rental, pointing in the direction of a dusty road across the street and shouting, *"Alla un restaurante bueno!"* He sticks out his hand, clamouring for payment for the morsel of information, *"Un peso, un peso."* Eda digs a ten-peso coin from her wallet and hands it to the kid. What the heck, we decide; let's give it a go. Unknown to us, we are following a trail that will lead me back to my curious quest for the bun.

At the end of the rutted road we find what we are looking for in an abandoned gold mine. Signs in the parking lot point us toward a forlorn brick edifice. Buoyed by approaching adventure, we hurry along a cobblestone walk and past a crumbling stone wall leading into the mine, oblivious to the danger posed by sagging beams, open shafts, and crumbling stairs that ascend to a restaurant called Escalera al Cielo, Stairway to Heaven. A local informs us that the operation is the brainchild of someone named Mark, who imagines reclaiming a portion of the town's former prosperity with a phoenix-rising-from-the-fire venture. We find our way inside and there he is, presiding over cash register, counter, and kitchen with the bearing of a king. When he turns around to lift a baking sheet of cinnamon buns from the oven, time stands still.

He passes them under our noses, awaiting our moans of delight, tantalizing us with their sweet warm smell. The gears in my brain jam as I try to process the simultaneous appearance of the two gorgeous specimens—the guy and the buns. Eda, quick to recognize my emotional disarray, grabs my arm and guides me to a table in the courtyard, where I can sit and regain my composure. I order a double margarita and she follows suit. Although Eda appears less stunned than me by the unlikely coupling of man and bun, I sense that the sighting of the man shakes her up as well. We knock back the first drink, order and polish off a second, and wait for our food to arrive.

Eda immediately dubs him the sexy Renaissance biker and we are confident in our assessment. In the sexy department, we trust our female instincts; regarding the Renaissance thing, what else can you call a dude who looks like that and bakes buns? And the biker thing? Well, that's easy, what with the tattoos, the fringed leather bolero that reveals his dark-haired chest, and the Harley we see parked at the entrance to the mine.

Throughout the meal and despite the fine Mexican fare, a good portion of my pleasure is eaten away by a persistent question about Mark's buns. *Should I partake or not?* Finally, I grab the horns of the dilemma and make my decision. The answer is a resolute "No." I cannot stomach the thought of eating a cinnamon bun on top of tortilla soup and chicken mole—either on principle or gastronomically. I choose the cardinal sin of omission and accept the consequences, which turn out to be somewhat dire, for in my decision I betray not only myself but also Antoinette Emily. I imagine her looking down at me from her stairway to Heaven, incredulous that her daughter has failed to act on her convictions. I feel like Casey at the bat when he strikes out in Mudville. There is no joy for any of us. The saga of the Mexican bun ends badly.

By the time we drive through the outskirts of La Paz with its pretty, meandering boardwalk, I start to feel a nagging discomfort like heartburn, but suspect that the sensation will not be easily remedied. I suffer an affliction related to *hambre del alma*, soul hunger, which is a matter of gravitas that requires something stronger than TUMS or a homeopathic tincture to cure my loss of the bun that got away. The unhappy experience stays with me well past my return to Canada, niggling me for more than a year before I determine to right the wrong.

Opportunity arrives in the fall of 2013 when Sarah phones to say she is coming home from Vancouver for the weekend. Hearing her plans, I have a sudden idea of my own. I know exactly how to carpe diem. "Great!" I exclaim, "I'd like to take you on a short trip before coming home. I'll catch the first morning ferry and meet you in Horseshoe Bay."

She balks. "Why the panic? Why six o'clock in the morning?"

"Trust me," I cajole. "We'll need to start early and be on time. Arriving ten minutes late could make the difference between triumph and failure."

The trip across Howe Sound from the Sunshine Coast is smooth sailing. I drive my car off the ferry and up to the curb, where Sarah flags me down and hops in. She greets me with a hasty hello and a kiss and we are off. By 7:30 I have settled into driving up the winding Squamish Highway, with the ocean a treacherous drop to our left and a fearsome rock wall threatening us on our right. Still, I am woman on a mission and pleased as punch about our morning adventure. Along the way I hum, *Non, rien de rien. Non, je ne regrette rien.*

Sarah, on the other hand, is still in the dark about my plan and remains unconvinced. "Where are we going?" she asks suspiciously.

"We're going to Whistler."

"Whistler?" she snorts. "Why?"

My guile does not fool her; a second later she yelps. "We're going to Whistler—to Ciao Thyme—for cinnamon buns!" She has my number and I allow her a laugh at my expense.

"Yup," I reply smoothly, careful not to betray my eagerness that increases the closer we get to our destination.

"We're going for the buns. We should arrive about the time they're coming out of the oven."

As we reach the town limits, I spell out my plan. "When we get within striking distance of the café I'll stop and let you park the car." Shortly after, I jump out and sprint down the sidewalk. Sarah assumes the driver's seat. A moment later I burst into the café, pausing briefly to catch my breath and assess the situation. I move quickly to position myself in front of the counter. In truth there is no lineup per se, but I am not going to be sloppy and lose my place. Besides, I am certain that a lineup will form soon enough, and I am correct. Within minutes the number of folks waiting for hot cinnamon buns swells to a good-sized group: snowboarders, executive couples, smart young families, backpackers travelling solo. Feeling the pressure of the line building behind me, I take charge and ask the winsome blonde standing behind the counter the question that's on everyone's mind.

"Are the buns out of the oven yet?"

She calculates carefully, "I'd say, give them five more minutes." As an afterthought she tacks on an explanation, an apology of sorts: "The cook got a late start this morning." Her comment spreads along the line.

Sarah joins me. We wait with the others in exquisite expectation, like a crowd of well-wishers outside Buckingham Palace, hoping for a glimpse of a new royal baby. Finally, the cook pulls a pan of buns from the oven and sets it down on the counter with a clatter. I stand riveted at the sight. The group leans toward the counter in a single action, flushed with anticipation, but

the cook—experienced in matters of crowd control—
decrees, "They'll have to cool for a few minutes." A
groan issues from the line. We strain against the obstacle
like penned animals, exhibiting signs of growing irritation and restlessness. The wait is unbearable. So close
and yet so far away—almost enough to spoil the adventure. In due time the cook announces, "Okay, okay," and
we lurch forward in a tight, determined queue. No one is
going to barge into our line.

I grab the power of my position. "I'll take two. Two
buns," I state, nudging Sarah with my elbow to alert her
to our moment of triumph. We grab the small white boxes
with the warm buns nestled inside and make a dash for the
door. With the Mexican mishap still fresh in my mind I'm
taking no chances, but Sarah has caught the mood. "Ciao,
ciao," she calls over her shoulder as we step across the
threshold and into the frigid morning. Her comment tick-
les my fancy and prompts me to mark the moment myself.

I raise my voice like an orator. "This is cause for cele-
bration!" With that, I retrieve my bun from the box and
raise it high in the air. Sarah mimics my movements. We
wave our buns, toast the occasion with solemn ceremony
and brandish them like trophies.

The sweetness is immeasurable.

The pleasure is ours for the tasting.

And the last words are mine.

"Carpe diem. Seize the day. And *now*—let's eat the bun!"

4

THE

COAT

———

IT IS A mystery how this departure from our family's careful ways came about, but here I am—ten years old—standing at the post office wicket next to my mother, who is holding a white Canada Post parcel card and what I quickly discover is a money order for ninety-nine dollars. *Ninety-nine dollars?* I almost faint. She is about to hand over ninety-nine dollars. She turns to me and says simply, "It's for a coat."

A voice inside my head croaks, *Ninety-nine dollars? Ninety-nine dollars for a coat?* My world shifts as I witness the stunning moment. Shortly after, I watch her unwrap the brown paper package on the dining room table and lift out a long, black, luxurious coat made from what she calls faux fur—something modern and exotic in 1958. For all I know, it is a full-length, dark mink made from the finest female skins, but it is clear to me that she loves the coat, and I can see why. She is gorgeous in the thing—walks and looks like a queen in it—and she wears it for years, meaning it owes her nothing. Ultimately, it ends up made over by my mother as a man-style throw, folded at the foot of our father's bed: a plush blanket backed with grey wool. Through my mother I learn firsthand: coats have the power to enhance or destroy a woman's sense of self.

THE STAGE WAS set. If you have lived in the frozen north, which I did for my first seventeen years, or if you live on the sodden West Coast of British Columbia, which I have done for the past twenty-five years, coats are a fact of life.

When I was a young girl, the topic of coats had already taken hold with me—its presence bolstered by the fact that I came from a sewing family. Four generations of women reached back to the early 1800s—either renowned seamstresses or simply excellent sewers, as in the case of my mother, who made all our clothes, including coats, when my sister, Joann, and I were growing up. For these craftswomen, coats and clothing were woven into their beings. My interest was inevitable, my psyche an unwitting carrier of the family gene passed from them to me and deposited in my DNA. Furthermore, I grew up absorbing messages about the significance of coats. Our mother had the definitive word on the subject. She told Joann and me repeatedly, "A good coat covers a multitude of sins." This sweeping statement gave us licence to wear shorts under our coats in the summer when we went to church, making it easier to run outside once the service was over; licence to wear pyjamas under our coats when we caught the overnight Canadian National train to Prince George for our dentist appointments, making it easier to slide into the drop-down bunks in the roomette and settle in for the night. Our mother's words also inferred the saving grace of a good coat, if one had the misfortune of finding herself in a hospital wearing less-than-lovely clothes underneath. Early on, I learned lesson number one: a good coat makes a positive first impression.

But her statement about a multitude of sins? Well, that confused me. Who was she kidding? Was she suggesting in a weird way that our clothes were awful? Or did this apply only to other people? People who bought their clothes through the Sears mail-order catalogue? But whatever she meant, from where I stood there was nothing bad or sinful about the clothes she made for us. Just the opposite. Our clothes were beautiful, like exhibits in the annual fall fair, worthy of the Best in Show category. I loved it all, right down to the colour and feel of the fabric—which she let us choose sometimes—to the tucks, contrasting trim, self-covered buttons and satin bows. Without exception, the clothes she sewed for us and the clothes we wore were always identical. We never questioned that. Dressing like my sister, who was one year older, made me feel safe—like I knew where I belonged in our family. Pictures snapped some sixty years ago captured these wonderful garments, which rightly could have been called children's couture.

The coats stood in a class all their own: wool tartan coats with black velvet Peter Pan collars and rows of round brass buttons; pale blue parkas with brown rabbit-fur trim on the hoods and leather belt buckles; brocade dusters with mandarin collars and single, silk-wrapped toggles at the neck. Our grandmother Nan, a renowned seamstress, born and apprenticed in England in the late 1800s before setting sail for Canada in 1911, made our dolls identical dusters, just like our own, lined and all.

In elementary school I thought little about coats. I knew ours were different than our friends' coats, but so were our clothes. In the summer before I entered grade seven and junior high, I knew that, come fall, I would be screwing up my nerve and asking for a store-bought winter coat—a request close to heresy in our home, but no worse than what Joann wanted. Joann wanted her braids cut off before she started grade eight. Shortly after, I piggybacked on her plan and pushed in alongside her as she approached our mother with the request to be shorn of our locks. Curiously, our mother put up no argument and lopped them off silently with sharp dressmaker scissors one summer afternoon, while our father was out of town working on the Canadian National Railway. Before placing the braids carefully in a circular leather case, our mother tied matching ribbons on the ends and gave them to us to hold. They felt heavy and foreign in our hands, and we passed them back to her to put away in the leather case and into her old cedar chest, where they remain. For a brief time, the idea of broaching a store-bought winter coat took on less urgency.

For Joann, cutting off her braids announced a water-shed moment—a demarcation between life as a girl and that of a young woman. Before long, she cast off the matching clothes and her younger-by-a-year sister at the same time, untangling herself from our shared identity.

The braid ceremony left no doubt about the success of the operation, but the store-bought winter coat—once we got around to it—failed to live up to its allure, provoking only irritation and a sense of betrayal. It lacked the elegance I longed for and I hated the colour. The brown wool fabric was bulky and stiff; the collar offensive and ugly—a wide, bias-cut, wraparound affair buttoned to one side. Still, I wore it for two winters, which was the deal in our home. Two years, like it or not, although I wondered whether my mother knew how I felt. If she did, she never breathed a word, never gloated how a store-bought coat would always be inferior. But the experience taught me lesson number two: buying a coat is a worrisome proposition.

By the time I completed my unhappy stint with the brown coat, our mother had reached a new level of autonomy unheard of in our home. After the mail-order coat, our mother ultimately made a second extravagant purchase, and the next time it was for me. I was fifteen years old when I saw a jacket in the window of Eva's Fashions on Main Street in Smithers, while walking home from school. When we returned the following day, my mother approached Eva at the counter, leaned toward her, and spoke quietly. I stood back watching as Eva slipped it off the mannequin and passed it to me to try. Seeing me zipped and cozy inside the darling jacket, my mother declared, "It's absolutely you," and promptly laid down eighty-five dollars to buy it. *Eighty-five dollars?* Her boldness, her aplomb, her *je-ne-sais-quoi* flair took my breath away, but she didn't bat an eye. She clearly appreciated—like daughter, like mother—its style and sophistication, and the fabric with its surprising splashes of red, black, and white that looked like a shower of confetti.

The two unlikely purchases clinched an unspoken understanding between us, fashioning a perfect match of sensibility and proclivity. The coat had worked its way into our psyches.

But the winning coat was the one my mother bought me in my first year at Simon Fraser University, in 1965, when I was seventeen years old. Exactly why she bought it I did not know, given the outrageous price tag. Maybe she bought it because she knew I was desperately homesick, too young to be away from home, alone in a dormitory with one hundred other girls, depressed even though we had no word for what I was feeling. Or because I gained weight eating cafeteria food and lost all sense of myself as a fine athlete. Regardless of her reasons, that winter she bought me an emerald green wool coat trimmed with genuine fox fur that swirled around the cuffs and hemline. A coat so extravagant as to befit a Russian princess. It was clear. The coat had lured my mother and me into extreme behaviour.

One weekend during my first semester I flew to Calgary to visit Joann, who met me at the airport dressed in a lightweight jacket, despite the sub-zero temperature. She almost fainted when I stepped from the plane wearing the princess coat. Something was wrong with the picture, she knew it implicitly, yet could not put her finger on it. But perhaps she was the luckier one—neither caught up nor affected by the curious web my mother and I shared.

After that visit, the drama in the coat department settled down considerably. Coats became a non-issue for almost forty years, until my daughter, Sarah, entered her junior year at Occidental College in Los Angeles and needed a coat. Suddenly the matter of coats no longer simmered on the back burner as a latent issue, but instead became the impetus behind Joann and me visiting Sarah in the fall of 2010. I arrived in California as a mother on a mission. Joann became a bystander, willing to participate in a marginal way, but unwilling to be drawn into the intensity of the search. Mainly she drove the rental car to various stores while Sarah and I plotted our course through the streets of Los Angeles.

Mid-afternoon on our first day shopping we hit the treasure trove at REI, a sporting goods store where after a minimum of trying and talking I stepped up—smart and quick—and bought her two coats: a snappy rain jacket in burgundy and fuchsia and a trendy all-weather coat in a fitted Lululemon style, sage green with a sturdy zipper and a hood. Sporty and practical: smart casual. Both fit like a damn and looked great on her. My mission was complete. For the rest of the weekend we enjoyed a more mellow mood. I could finally breathe, slow and deep, as the adrenalin drained from my body. Imagining Sarah dry and warm kept me content for almost a year.

BUT TEN MONTHS later and during a blissful July and August, hubris convinces me that I can kick my ten-year dependency on prescription drugs for anxiety and insomnia; tells me I don't need doctors; urges me to toss out my meds. Summer 2011, with its playful ways and charming fantasies, surrenders reluctantly to the wrath of fall. Reality hits hard. Unending rain, ferocious wind, black waves heaving themselves over the boulders surrounding my property, depositing greasy wood, plastic bottles, beer cans, and Styrofoam onto my lawn. An *episode* looms with the changing season. This year is no different—only worse—without the chemicals.

Anxiety—like a parasite, like a toxic intruder—returns to collect its toll, spew a nasty spiking energy through my system, attach itself to a willing host, which it finds in my obsessive mind, which in turn latches onto the subject of coats, dismissed months ago following my successful spree with Sarah. But it returns—like the ghost of Jacob Marley, rattling its chains—to declare *it is me* who needs a coat. After living on the West Coast for over two decades, the gig is up and buying a raincoat is no longer optional.

Once the search is on, a familiar pattern takes up residency in my mind. High-pitched anxiety spins me into a dervish of energy during the day and traps me in a frantic insomnia at night. I need to put myself out of my misery. Desperation is the reason I capitulate and drive myself to see a psychiatrist who prescribes a new round of drugs to straighten me out—but not before I end up buying a brilliant, overpriced, waxy-gold polyester raincoat with a hood, although I have hated hoods for years.

I break in the coat by walking on the beach in encroaching darkness, but when I venture out in public I cringe with shame to be seen wearing the thing. Still, I get what I ask for when I promise myself, "I'll wear anything, even gold—but not black!" And black it is not. Gold it is.

BY CHRISTMAS 2011 the drugs kick in. I'm putting the final touches on bundles of shortbread cookies that I will deliver to friends, clients, and people I volunteer with. Each ribbon-wrapped gift bears a handwritten note.

Dozens. I make dozens of these thank-you packages every year, still convinced that a personalized gift outshines a singing greeting sent by email. But after days of cutting and baking, I am *done* with the stars, trees, bells, and angels. Not exactly bored, but I want to be finished. I chafe at the idea of wrapping even one more bundle, but I know that six perfect angels wait quietly on the cookie sheet for my attention.

"Oh, what the hell," I mutter, as I wrap the last of them. This is the only bundle without a card. And there's only one person I've missed this year. Ruth, an elf of a woman who lives alone with her old dog, Babe.

"Can I be bothered?" I groan, but an inner twinge overrides my uncharitable thought. I select a card and prepare Ruth's cookies, my mood softening as I do.

It's a wild wet day. I grab my golden coat and the bundles of cookies, and head outside to my car. I'll start with Ruth, who lives closest to me.

Minutes later I'm standing at her door. I ring the bell, my hood pulled over my head to protect me from the rain.

Babe yips as Ruth opens the door inch by inch. Wonder lights her face when she sees me dressed in my splendour.

"A golden angel at my door," she whispers, her voice filled with emotion, barely audible. She pulls me into the house and wraps her arms around me, moaning and sniffling as she continues, "And I thought God had forgotten me this Christmas! And here you are—my own golden angel." I grin and flap my angel arms.

"I have a surprise for you," I announce, extending my arm and placing the bundle in her hand. "Go on, open it."

"Oh my, oh my," she says, her hand touching her heart as she beholds the angels lying in cellophane wrap. For Ruth and me, this is Christmas—in one shining moment.

FIVE YEARS HAVE passed since Ruth and the golden coat. Winter solstice 2016 and the darkest day of the year, I arrive at noon with fellow parishioners from the Anglican Church to volunteer at our annual food bank event. Recently retired from real estate and after a five-year hiatus from baking and delivering bundles of shortbread cookies, I return to my tradition, anticipating the delight of giving these gentle expressions of love and appreciation as if I were receiving them myself. For Muriel, our music director, a choir of angels; for Rosemary, a former client and fine soprano who sings next to me, a cluster of shortbread hearts; and for Jonah, our new vicar, who will not condone decorations on a tree before Christmas Eve, his own small forest of evergreens, natural and unadorned like trees in Robert Frost's woods on a snowy evening.

After weeks of canvasing, collecting, packaging, and organizing, the day arrives when we hand out our hampers in the church hall and open our hearts to folks in town who need it most. Rows of tables sag under heaps of food donated by local merchants, along with piles of toiletries and sundry items from our big-box drug store: socks, gloves, and scarves, packs of men's Jockey underwear, lace lingerie, Almond Roca, Lindt chocolate, Kerr's toffees, scented candles, and Santa hats. Our guests shiver outside, waiting for the doors to open, imagining the warmth of a crackling fire and feelings of comfort and joy. Finally, a blast of air ushers them in and a visitor, unannounced, enters. It is my mother—long deceased—dropping in for a visit, dressed in the same simple blue garment she wore in a recent dream.

Visible only to me, she pauses at the entrance; bright eyes sweep the room before she finds me positioned at my table handing out used blankets, sleeping bags, crocheted afghans, winter boots, and clothes. Within seconds, I feel her arms around me. Silence holds us in a still embrace. As in the dream, we communicate mind to mind. We require no words after a lifetime together.

Like watching wheels turn, I see her register a thought as she notices my quilted North Face coat, now in its seventh winter and the once-rich colour called "mission fig" noticeably faded. A grin lights her face and we laugh when we see that the exacting standards of style we once shared are a thing of the past.

She steps back briefly, then comes closer again to peer at a large paper clip dangling off the zipper.

What's this? she asks, flicking the paper clip with an index finger.

I reply without words. *Sarah's solution to the broken pull tab on my zipper.*

Her eyes dance with delight and a chuckle reverberates between mother and daughter. A single word forms in her mind: *Ingenious.*

She pauses to savour the moment and expand the thought. *My granddaughter, the girl I never knew when I was alive. Ingenious.*

Turning to leave and looking ever so slightly puffed with pride—her face radiant with joy—she stops, waves, and exits the hall.

5

THE

DANCE

THE YEAR IS 1955. I am seven years old when something awakens in me long before I know the meaning of a word like transcendence. My first encounter with the dance is on a grassy stage overlooking the Bulkley River near my home in Smithers, British Columbia.

I practise with a small group of girls at wooden bars set up around the living room walls of my dance teacher's home, rehearsing for a ballet recital. Our teacher doesn't talk much about the plans, how we will dance one dusky summer evening at Herbert's Farm, so close to town yet never visited or imagined. Nor does she tell us about colours or costumes. But suddenly things move fast and here we are at Herbert's Farm. I am the girl dressed in the chartreuse tutu.

How did this happen? How was I chosen to wear this exquisite colour—so beautiful it dazzles my eyes?

A magical landscape stretches beyond me. Faraway mountains wrap around a verdant valley. Pink alpenglow sweeps the sky, and wonder stirs inside me.

Is this Heaven? Are other girls dancing with me? Is my mother watching, her face turned toward the turf stage?

I cannot say. It is my own ecstatic moment and the genesis of something more powerful than I can understand. This is where it begins.

BY 1960, LIFE in my family—my mother, father, me, and my sister, Joann—reverberates with change. I am twelve years old and have just entered junior high; my braids are a thing of the past; our mother starts teaching school again; and we move to a new post-and-beam house, built by a European craftsman in a new area of town that locals call "The Hill." Our father buys our first television and an impressive cabinet-style stereo set. The units arrive shortly after we move into the new house, delivered one afternoon by two burly men who install them in the living room. With these unlikely purchases, new characters, voices, and energy flood our home.

I marvel at what forces conspire to bring Ed Sullivan and The Beatles directly into our living room the first time they appear on U.S. television. For the occasion I wear a blue Banlon sweater with gold appliquéd butterflies. I remember it all, like I remember the first man landing on the moon five years later. Both events, pivotal and miraculous, proffer a giant leap into a larger world. But the sight and sound of The Beatles in our living room trumped the man on the moon.

Who would believe that the stereo set—with its record player and radio—would open surprising new vistas and bring us a wider range of music than the two stereophonic records by Carmel Quinn and Frankie Laine that our father plays repeatedly? But between the television and the stereo set—however remarkable they both are—the stereo wins hands down and establishes my life on a vivid course.

Aside from these startling events Joann and I are coming to grips with, nothing prepares us for what follows: the way the stereo—along with our new house with its larger kitchen—sets the scene for dancing to slip in and claim centre stage in our home.

With our mother back teaching, Joann and I have the responsibility for starting dinner before she comes home. It is always a flurry—peeling potatoes and boiling them on the stove, scrubbing carrots to put on later, making sure we are ready when she arrives, and the added pressure of knowing that our father will show up at any moment, but never knowing what to expect when he does. It happens like this on any given day.

He's home. We hear him whistling outside before we actually see him. When he opens the kitchen door he marches straight into the living room and turns on the new stereo, without as much as a word of hello. When CBC Radio brings us big band music with Lawrence Welk or Lester Lanin, the house erupts.

He bursts into the kitchen and grabs me if I'm the closest, shouting out the words, "Let's dance!" He's already sweeping me around the floor—the potatoes boiling on the stove and Joann watching nearby. Then it's her turn and off they go around the kitchen. "Pick up your feet!" he barks. "Hold in your stomach!"

Mesmerized, I'm half-afraid and half-excited. But when I dance with him, the stiffness I usually feel evaporates like steam from the pot on the stove. As Joann and I begin high school and gain greater independence, dancing in the kitchen continues, still when we least expect it—between dates, basketball tournaments, track and field meets, fall fair projects, and parties. With my father and me, dancing is the only time we touch.

Even so, the effect of dancing with him always transports me to a sublime place where I understand that words are not required. Several years elapse before I dance with him again. When I do, it is at Joann's wedding. Calgary, 1968.

THE CEREMONY IS over. The photographer paces the steps of the red brick Catholic church, arranging us in straight-line form and clearly defined groups. Bride and groom, bridal party, family of the bride, family of the groom, family and others. He snaps his photographs, our faces turned west toward the foothills of the Rockies, the late summer sun blasting us with unseasonal heat.

Joann at twenty-one is darling and ethereal, covered in white satin and lace. I'm her bridesmaid, younger by a year. Standing next to her I'm startling and bold, all legs and limbs—a bronzed Amazon. My orange satin dress covers me only as far as wedding propriety requires; my long dark hair becomes an elaborate headdress with yellow rosebuds nestled in their own separate curls.

The photographs are finished; the wedding party and guests move next door to the church hall. The reception begins; dinner comes and goes. Telegrams are read, glasses clinked, and the bride kissed when the band begins playing, which alerts us to the first dance. The groom gathers his bride into his arms and onto the floor. It is like The Platters themselves are singing.

Only you can make all this world seem right . . .

Our parents join them for the second dance, their movements fluid and graceful. A third song begins and my father walks toward me. "Come on, Pat," he says, his voice catching with emotion. "Let's dance." Suddenly we're gliding, drifting, floating. The hall, the carpet, white linen cloths, crepe-paper bells, the wedding guests, and the EXIT sign recede and dissolve. All that exists is the dance and the muted sound of my father whistling.

Is it right to dance with my father most of the night? Is it fair to my mother, sitting on the sidelines, dignified and beautiful in a red silk dress?

I cannot say. The thought never enters my mind.

THROUGHOUT MY TWENTIES and thirties, dancing becomes an irrepressible force, the twists and turns reflecting the changing partners, the ups and downs of life. The spark ignited as a seven-year-old girl in a chartreuse tutu burns brighter and hotter. Dancing brings its own brand of eroticism that sets my brain and body on fire. My response is instinctual, visceral. Dancing is the way I tease out information about a man as a potential lover. His smell, his touch, his pleasure in his own body, his sense of authority as he holds me close.

I dance around a lot during this time: in clubs and civic centres, in ballrooms and barns. But dancing is coquettish—like a trickster—full of delights and disappointments. Scenes from over the years rush forward.

Dancing to The Righteous Brothers playing live at The Cave in Vancouver—the hottest ticket in town—with my friend Harry. The year is 1965. We're students at Simon Fraser University. I'm wearing a posh, aqua satin cocktail dress, which I made myself during the Christmas holidays: empire waist, A-line skirt, and a fine row of self-covered buttons down the bodice. We press together on the dance floor, never missing a beat or a song all night. The mirrored ball rotates overhead in languid loops, showering our bodies with shards of silver light. The next day he sends red roses to my dorm but, sadly, I never did have that loving feeling for him. Still, the night ranks as a stellar evening of dance.

Dancing as a young teacher in Calgary with my live-in boyfriend, Lyle, 1973. We're at the civic centre, a cavernous building that functions as an ice rink in winter and party palace during off-season. But the drab surroundings do not stop me from feeling hot in a red velvet jersey jumpsuit with bell bottoms and a lace tie that runs between my navel and cleavage. I look like Elvis's bride. Lyle is no longer dancing—no longer living, in fact—but he loved me enough to dance with me to Stevie Nicks and Fleetwood Mac, and Meat Loaf himself, who, despite his uncouth appearance, has something noteworthy to say. And I don't disagree with him. Most things considered, two out of three ain't bad.

Dancing in a barn in 1981 at a small-town rodeo, my partner a lanky young cowboy with dusty jeans, scuffed boots, and a great grin. Blame it on the sexy music for the difference it makes, but the night gets away on me. The next morning the words *stand by your man, and show the world you love him* stick like straw in my brain. I forget his name but I remember his moves. I admit it. The whole affair, stripped of its hokey gloss, is a misstep. But the next time I dance at a rodeo, it's a big deal. The Calgary Stampede, 1985: The Greatest Outdoor Show on Earth.

This time I'm at a posh party at a house on the Elbow River with my friend Sonja. Rhinestone cowgirls in silk and leather, tooled boots, ornate belts, and Sonja with a small fan of feathers on her hat brim. I see him manoeuvre his way through the raucous crowd until he's smack in front of me. His face suggests that he recognizes me, but all I know is that he's a handsome man in a cowboy hat. Dispensing with introductions, he grabs me in his arms and kisses me. Only then does he tell me his name is Brian. We dance most of the night away to one western song after another.

And it's sad to be alone
Help me make it through the night . . .

Swept away as I am by this man, I see no reason why I shouldn't do exactly that.

The crowd thins out; we're hot and sweaty from dancing. I grab his hand and lead him away from the party to my car. I pause at the door, unlock it, turn, and look at him directly.

"Love me," I say, "long and slow."

I hop in, drive off, and leave him with a smile and a wave.

'Cause I am your lady
And you are my man . . .

He follows closely behind.

Early in our relationship I use the word *inevitable* and so it is. We marry a year later. In 1989, just days before my forty-first birthday, our beautiful daughter, Sarah, is born, fulfilling the promise of the dance with love, marriage, and wondrous new beginnings.

OUR MARRIAGE LASTS ten years but ultimately frays beyond repair. Even dancing in a German castle—with me wearing a silk sheath and gorgeous golden shoes and Brian dressed in a fine wool tuxedo—cannot put us back together again. Once we return home, the dancing stops altogether. By the time we separate we are living in Gibsons, a small coastal community in British Columbia, forty minutes on a ferry from West Vancouver.

In curiously quick succession after my last dance with Brian, I have a second last dance, this one with my father, who has died six months earlier. He appears to me in a dream, in a dance hall in Heaven, arriving on cue to "The Great Pretender," a Platters song from the fifties and a favourite in our home as we were growing up. I call the dream "My Father."

> *The instant the orchestra strikes the opening notes I know the song and rush to find my father, to draw him out from where he stands among the shadows.*
> Oh yes, I'm the great pretender
> Pretending that I'm doing well . . .
> *We begin to dance, our bodies touching; moving with a natural ease. A seamless waltz of words and music holds us enraptured—dancing on a precipice between two worlds. I sense that his knees hurt and I love him all the more, for coming like this to see me. The song fades and he speaks on his own behalf. "You have a beautiful figure," he declares, then disappears.*

His words, straightforward and simple, reveal what he is unable to say while still alive. Our relationship has come full circle. We are blessed by the healing grace of the dance.

AFTER THESE LAST dances, first with my husband and then with my father, I dance around a lot less, not from a lack of desire but a dearth of partners. Dancing is relegated to backstage in my life. Still, some bright moments stand out.

Dancing one hot summer night in 2003 at a barge party in Vancouver. I'm fifty-five years old, wearing tight jeans and showing off my tan with a strapless white stretch top. I stand along the side of a rough plank floor, scanning the crowd and watching couples dance. My eyes lock with a handsome fellow clear across the floor. We nod in mutual consent and begin walking toward the other. The dance galvanizes, pulls us together without preamble or words. We meet somewhere in the middle of the floor. We pick up the beat and dance like we've been partners for years.

Richard, an investment banker from San Francisco, is in Vancouver on business, but it is dancing that determines where we go from here. Ever generous and gracious, after the barge party he accepts my invitation to a dance in a nearby coastal community. He arrives after a day of travel by plane, taxi, and ferry, tired but eager to waltz me around the seniors' centre, a million miles from the glamour of a world-class city. Richard wears a black tuxedo with a formal white shirt open at the neck; I wear a long, bias-cut jersey dress that clings and swirls as I move.

Inspired by our weekend together he imagines us dancing at the Top of the Mark in San Francisco, but, ultimately, our plans prove too extravagant for what will become only marginal romantic returns.

By 2008 Joann and I take dancing matters into our own hands and sign up for a tango cruise through the Mediterranean. We board the ship in Venice like innocents bound for slaughter, oblivious to the pain of blistered feet, aching backs, and the humiliation that awaits us. Instead the tango beguiles us with throbbing music, imaginary whiffs of danger, and illusions of dancing with exotic strangers as we travel from Italy, through the Greek islands, to Dubrovnik and back. But the reality of the cruise is drastically different.

After four or five agonizing hours of lessons each day—wrapping our brains and contorting our bodies around the complicated moves of the tango—we return night after night to the *milonga*, or tango party, wearing hopeful smiles and sultry dresses, offering ourselves like lambs at the altar of the dance. Yet night after night, we endure the indignity of feeling like wallflowers—at sixty and sixty-one years of age. None of the men in the tango group want to dance with beginners, and when they do, it is half-hearted—only to fulfill the obligation they agree to when they sign on to the cruise, which is to dance with the single ladies in exchange for a discounted price. We reel with shame. Our mother would have called this adding insult to injury.

AFTER THE TANGO setback, dance disappears from my life. Three uneventful years pass before I encounter a dark stranger in a black shirt at a local club in Gibsons—when the lure of the dance returns in a flash.

Dancing with the handsome stranger, my mind races. I picture myself lying in bed with this *hunk, a hunk of burning love.* And you bet, like this song that our friend, Jimmy, is singing, I would happily waltz across Texas with this dude, still wearing the same black dress with its slits and slashes and soft sheer panel over the bodice and down the back. So sleek and smooth it would have been criminal to wear underwear.

This is slow dancing at its best: full-body contact and creative use of some of the sexier moves borrowed from the tango. I wrap my left leg around his right, slip down—ever so slightly—to ride his beautiful thigh, dancing as we go, and me feeling friskier than I have in years. The fact that he dances off with another partner later in the evening bruises my ego, but I know that something more important has happened. Dancing with the dark stranger is the force I need to rouse me from slumber, sweep me back into libido and life. I reawaken to a new, unfettered self.

In 2013 I take *life* matters into my own hands with a three-month winter sabbatical in San Miguel de Allende, Mexico. Exploring my own rhythm and accountable to no one, I study Spanish, show up Saturday mornings for a Zumba class in a nearby park, walk miles each day on cobblestone streets, careful not to twist an ankle or trip into a hazardous hole on the sidewalk, and practise patchy Spanish wherever I go. One evening I am having dinner with a new friend, a woman from school.

When we leave the restaurant it's surprisingly cold. We part with a quick hug and head home in different directions. Turning the corner onto my street, I hear the music before I see the open doorway and find myself standing on the threshold of La Valentina Buffet Mexicano. I'm the only *gringa* in sight, *pero no importa*. What *is* important are the two Mexican brothers singing, *She loves you, yeah, yeah, yeah* . . .

I take one look and want to join in. They see my excitement; their broad smiles invite me to sing along, and I do. I follow their lead, lifting my voice to blend with their fine tenors, all the while hanging back a short distance away in the doorway. The crowd loosens up as the brothers sing one round of favourites from the sixties and seventies after another, never stopping for a beer or a breather. Tips flow; they break into a Nancy Sinatra song.

Hearing the words *these boots are made for walking* sends a jolt of energy through my body. Restraint flies out the door. In a second, I leap from my perch and stride into the restaurant, kicking my tall black Italian boots out in front of me, stamping my feet as I *walk all over you*. The boots tell the story we've heard a hundred times. I strut past families eating *sopa de tortilla*, *flautas con puerco*, *frijoles negros*, *enchiladas verdes*—around tables and through the crowded restaurant. Much later I reach for my coat, wave goodbye to the brothers, and disappear into the night, laughing all the way home. The next morning I remember that sometime during my doorway dancing I turned sixty-five.

SHORTLY AFTER I return home from Mexico, Joann and I join a group of friends who buy tickets to a Saturday night dance at the local Legion, the only place in town that still allows smoking and caters to veterans and locals who like cheap booze and billiards. But the main reason we are at the Legion is that Jimmy is singing tonight and we are ready to dance. Most of the usual men hanging around the hall don't seem like the dancing types—which leaves me and my friends without partners, not counting two male friends and a couple of strangers whom we take turns dancing with.

One friend is a courtly eighty-year-old gentleman named Ian, who, despite being hard of hearing and having poor eyesight, is an animated dancer. Fortune is on my side when it's my turn to dance with him at the precise moment that Jimmy begins singing, *Crying over you . . .*

Ian offers his hand and leads me briskly to the floor. We're swaying to the music when he utters a sound of dismay.

"What's wrong?" I ask, fearing the worst.

"My hearing aid," he replies. "I've lost it." By now he's bent over and groping on the floor for the tiny device. For me, time is a-wasting. My response is quick and sure.

"Oh, don't cry," I implore, half seriously, half in jest. "You don't need your hearing aid to dance. Besides," I say, louder than usual, "you've got rhythm." This settles him down, helps him forget about his hearing aid, and allows us to finish without further mishap. The dance over, Ian walks me gallantly back to my seat beside Joann and sets forth to find his next partner.

The time between dances, however, creates an opportunity to observe different couples on the floor. One in particular catches our attention—a recently married elderly couple whose dancing is as smooth as their appearance is elegant. The woman wears a long, mauve, diaphanous dress that looks stunning with her silver hair, but it's her high, strappy, matching mauve shoes that impress me most.

Joann, watching them intently, leans toward me and whispers, "Do you think they're still having sex?"

"Of course, they're having sex," I retort. "They're dancing, aren't they?"

AS FOR ME, the dance continues to evoke its familiar longings—like a siren with her promises of pleasure.

Oh, my love, my darling
I've hungered for your touch.

6

THE

GIFT

———

IN MANY WAYS I hardly knew him. Certainly, I knew nothing about what he called the backstory of the past thirty-seven years of his life. But I did know him, in one essential way. I knew him as a twenty-seven-year-old man who had once used the word *sacred* to describe our relationship and our lovemaking. I had heard the word—otherwise why would it still be buried in my brain decades later—like a beautiful barb: still hooking me, still driving an impulse in me toward him? At the time, however, the word held little meaning.

YEARS LATER I became aware that something more was compelling me, something I could only describe as sacred relationship, sacred sex. Not that I even knew what this was, but I knew that it existed and that it was possible—even essential—for me to create in my life. As a fifty-year-old woman, I wrote about this longing in my memoir, when my relationship with my partner had run dry.

Throughout our two years together, we skirted any emotional issue that would have forced us to become raw and real, and we skimmed along on the surface instead, enjoying a West Coast lifestyle of skiing, hiking, boating, and biking. While we shared intimacies, we were not intimate. At the end I knew that I could not create what I needed with him, and the vessel for the relationship wore thin and crumbled.

DURING THE FOURTEEN years that followed this relationship, neither sex nor the lure of sex entered my life—until this winter, when I found a card in my mailbox. The card was from a man named Andrew, whom I had known four decades ago. The same man I once shared an unforgettable connection with; the man who, as a twenty-seven-year-old lover, had called our relationship sacred.

The card arrived like a missive from space, with Andrew requesting a copy of my memoir and at the same time sending me greetings for my upcoming sixty-fourth birthday. But the story began much earlier, in 1965, when I was seventeen and standing in a long line with other first-year students at Simon Fraser University in Vancouver.

One by one, we approached the registration desk to provide our personal information and complete the paperwork required to confirm our admittance. As I gave my name and birth date, the young man behind me chuckled and remarked, "Hey, that's my birthday, too!" He introduced himself as Andrew. After that he visited me occasionally in the common room of my dormitory where, even if he had made a move toward me, there was little chance that I would have agreed. I was a virgin.

AFTER UNIVERSITY I didn't see him again for ten years, until we discovered that we were both living and work-ing in Calgary. Soon after, we became lovers, even living together for a few months. Our relationship took hold on a foundation of emotional intensity that included jeal-ousy, suspicion, and secrets simmering below the surface. But we also shared a sexual chemistry that I did not fully understand at the time. Inevitably, this fusion of elements created a perfect chemical match. And combust it did. One night I returned to our apartment after meeting a married man I had had an affair with for three years— before reconnecting with Andrew. Andrew met me at the door, explosive and yelling, "Where were you? Were you with that old fuck?"

Andrew was right. Although I had rationalized that there was nothing wrong with seeing this other man, I was fucking around—as surely as if I had been screw-ing him. Andrew cut through my flimsy excuse that we were only walking in a park. Before I realized what was happening, he grabbed me by the neck and shook me roughly; his fingers pressed hard and strong into my flesh. We slept in the same bed that night but did not make love. Instead of curling up naked next to the man I called my lover, I wore a pale yellow lace camisole and panties, imagining that the scant lingerie would protect me from the danger lurking in the bedroom.

The morning after, the superintendent changed the apartment lock at my request. I refused the extravagant flowers that Andrew sent to the concierge office of my building. We never spoke again. We were done. Until I received his card on what would be our sixty-fourth birthday.

CONTACT WAS RE-ESTABLISHED after years of silence. Andrew insisted that we communicate only in writing, and for a while I was willing to oblige. He sent emails while I preferred cards and letters sent through Canada Post, which made me feel provocative as I described my life on the West Coast. But all too soon, the process became irritating, even distressing. I imagined my beautiful cards soaring eastward across the country to his home in Ontario. He responded with sporadic messages and comments that ranged from capricious to guarded. One moment I felt him reaching toward me, the next moment he was pulling away. I moved in one direction only. Toward him. Ultimately, the messages of the two mediums tangled in the process. Following the thread of our communication became impossible.

But the truth was, Andrew *had* me—from the moment I received his birthday card and shortly after—when he used the word *sanctity* in an email, which reignited my longing for sacred relationship. As a younger man in his twenties, he had understood something I now hungered for, and my mind and body quickened—with no concern for safety or the memory of a dangerous night. I was aroused and I wanted him. My imagination ran unchecked with the idea that we could be together again as a couple and create sacred union.

My energy changed. I felt light and breezy, flirty and sexy—as if I had a secret. My coworkers noticed the difference, particularly the men. One fellow remarked, "Hey, Patricia, what's up with you?" I thought about Andrew incessantly. Where distance was created by time and space, my mind filled in the gaps. When it came to fanning my desire for him, I had no pride.

I had no pride when I framed a picture of him that I found in a box of old photos. No pride when I studied it, trying to read what I saw in his face, wondering who he was today, wondering what he looked like. I wanted him— in my home, in my bed. I had no pride at night when I told him, "I love you, Andrew." No pride in the morning when I imagined reaching for his body and whispering, "Good morning, darling." No pride when I repeated words like a mantra: "We say yes to love, we say thank you to Spirit," intoning the words to invoke my longings.

I wrote erotic poems that I did not send, but read instead to a friend sitting across from me at the dinner table. The words, once unleashed, staggered me. I added heat to my emotions and played songs from *Mamma Mia!* over and over. Blasted the music and belted out lyrics that urged Andrew to take a chance on me. I wondered if I were losing my grip.

A force, relentless and impersonal, bore down on me with the power of a tsunami. It existed in service of one thing only: the human soul. I felt mine forcing a rite upon me, a necessary transformation, as if to ensure its very survival. It demanded I admit that my carefully manicured life was not enough to satisfy my soul.

My soul sparked a desire to burn off the constraints of my life, to allow something ancient and sacred to emerge—something larger, more beautiful, and unfurled. As I recalled our sexual connection I conferred upon him the magical power to animate this transformation. Knowing I was in the grip of a force greater than me— triggered when I first heard from Andrew—I had already decided that if this were the crucible for sacred relationship, I would endure.

The weeks passed and winter turned into spring. All the while, my emotions burned on a high-octane fuel. With the possibility of rekindling our love, I believed that the presence I called Spirit had offered us a numinous gift. But while I needed no convincing that we could create sacred union, it was unclear what Andrew would do. His communication had gone cold.

I HAD NOT heard from him in over six weeks when, *gracias a Dios*, a dream granted me a reprieve from my fitful mind. My dreamer, whom I named *"La que sabe,"* she who knows, confirmed my hunch about him. I called the dream "The Holy Trust."

I encounter two unfamiliar men. One stands over to the left side, a distance away. He stands naked with an erection,

inviting me to have sex with him. I am not interested. A sec-
ond man stands closer although not directly in front of me. I
am confused about what he is telling me. Trying to make
sense of his story, I ask, "Are you married? Do you have
children?" Is that the problem? I wonder.

"No," he replies.

I notice his hesitation and think, What the heck, maybe
I should have sex with him regardless. But I quickly realize
that this cannot happen because there is no energy between
us. The connection is flat and drab like the dream and I
understand its meaning. Without a commitment to create
something sacred, the sex can only disappoint; can never
deliver the joy or the healing, or the growing together
toward the Divine, which is the promise of Spirit's gift.
This gift comes with strings attached. No holy trust. No holy
gift. That's the deal.

The dream forced me to concede that, between Andrew
and me, I might be the only one eager to open the gift.
My feelings swung between gnawing disappointment and
awe—that I finally had the answer to my question, *What
is sacred relationship, sacred sex?* That, in itself, was a wondrous gift of another sort. But my realization did little
to satisfy my body, which had awakened from a four-
teen-year sleep, ravenous and raging like a bear. I wanted
flesh and blood. I wanted Andrew. Then, *gracias a Dios*, I
received a second dream a few days later from *La que sabe*,
who knew of my sexual and spiritual longings. I called it
"Eros Revisited."

I behold the image of a phallus that exists—not as part of a man's anatomy, but as symbolic of the masculine, appearing in service to the feminine. The message is unequivocal. I am not afraid and allow the phallus to penetrate my body. I surrender to the pleasure, riding a wave of orgasm.

I awakened from the dream charged with the thrusting focused energy of the masculine, which flooded my body, forced me out of bed, and emboldened me to grab the story and get it down. After finishing, I lived in limbo for a few days, wondering, *What do I do next? Do I wait for a dream directive? Do I dare send this story to Andrew?*

I SENT IT to Andrew—as I have written it to this place in time. Receiving no response from him after two months, I called. "Did you get my story? What did you think?"

His response: non-plussed. "Flattering and fascinating," he said.

IT TOOK ME three years to get over Andrew. To expunge the fantasy of having him in my bed and in my life. To extract the barb embedded in me. The process began when I awakened one morning in a clammy bed with a sweaty sheet pressed against my face, by then a sixty-seven-year-old woman. An ache for what might have been pervaded my spirit. I lay in bed and felt my heart soften. The tears came, slid down my cheeks, slipped into my ears, mingled with the sweat on my sheets. Gone was the feeling of unbridled resolve that incited me back then to seize my will and write my own story to Andrew. At the time, this was my desperate measure to rouse a response from him and break the tension that had been building in me from the moment he initiated contact.

A few days later I realized that the storm that had pummelled me had passed. I could savour the stillness in the aftermath, incredulous that calm had returned to me and my world. I checked for injuries and found no blood, broken bones, or lacerations. The injuries were strictly internal: the shame of rejection, the hopelessness of unreturned love, and the loss of a dream to share sacred union with Andrew—all feelings I had been unable to admit until a few days ago. But the mayhem was over. My mind was finally released from the compulsive yearning for sacred relationship and my heart was ready to heal.

THE GIFT MEANT many things to me. Eros renewed my soul with life-giving energy and opened the way for a more compassionate, joyful, erotic self to return. The gift revealed that sacred relationship and sacred sex were only possible with a trust between partners to receive Spirit into the relationship. Equally importantly, and despite my sorrow, it allowed me to recognize something that I had not wanted to see about my relationships with men.

It was time for a conversation with myself. I asked, *What went wrong with Andrew?* and waited for a savvier part of myself to answer.

That savvy part was direct and her words drove to the point. *The way you came on to Andrew, you were unfurled all right. Blustery and full of yourself. But you know,* she continued, *Andrew was nothing more than a fantasy in your overheated imagination.*

Besides, what man wants a tsunami bearing down on him? Any man in his right mind would run for higher ground— never to be seen again.

She carried on, her voice strident with authority. *When it comes to men, let them come on to you. Let them turn up the heat. Remember, they're sensitive creatures, ready to retreat at any excuse.*

You mean easy does it? I asked like a sassy broad.

Something like that, she tossed off flippantly.

Still, I needed to speak on my own behalf. *I wanted Andrew to see me, not as a twenty-seven-year-old woman he had once known, but as a confident woman who was unafraid to express my desire for him and sacred union. In a way I was pushing him to reveal the man he had become—to determine whether a relationship with him could withstand the honesty required to forge a holy connection with Spirit. If I had been coy—like a girl—it would have been a lie and a betrayal of myself. Either way was risk. In response to his initial overture, I chose to be forthright and what I considered to be clever.*

Of course, you were clever, she interrupted. *Of course, you were clever,* she repeated, before pausing to temper her outburst and continue more gently. *Clever—but not very smart.*

I had to agree.

7

THE
TIPPING
POINT

READY OR NOT, *you must be caught*. Even if it means hauling oneself out of hiding, which is what I've done. First, by insisting that my family doctor refer me to a psychiatrist, and second, by showing up for an appointment with him after a four-month wait. Finally, I'm driven to settle the question that has plagued me for years: *Is something wrong with my brain?* And the other questions that rush in closely behind: *Is this real? Is this a matter of chemistry, hormonal imbalance? Or is this existential angst? Is my soul demanding that I wake up and see the light—change the direction of my life?* I'm constantly torn between these two possibilities. Worse yet, a question nags me without mercy: *Is my struggle—dare I say my suffering—all in my head?*

This last idea troubles me. Growing up in the fifties and sixties in small-town northern British Columbia, rule number one in our house is no snivelling. Yet here I am, no doubt nothing more than a middle-aged woman wanting sympathy and attention. In other words, *snivel-ling*. Thinking I've got something to complain about.

So I don't complain. Instead I remain silent about what is going on in my life, calling the emotional upheavals I experience *episodes*—a word slyer than it sounds and one that denies the treachery of what I battle on a recurring basis. I dance around more precise words that could nail the matter and put my questions to rest, once and for all.

My mind wanders to a series of books that delighted my daughter, Sarah, as a young girl. Written by a certain Lemony Snicket, they share a curious subtitle: *A Series of Unfortunate Events*. Snicket's words suit my mental antics and I call my own experiences "A Series of Unfortunate Episodes." But when I cut through the phrase, what I'm describing is dealing with bouts of *not being normal*. Call it what you will.

DURING THESE BOUTS I contend with Cerberus, the hound of hell, snapping at my heels, keeping me vigilant and wary, on the lookout for when he will strike again. Any reprieve I feel is tenuous at best, deceptive at worst—lulling me into believing there is nothing wrong with me. But who knows when he will drag me down again? Black and blue and red all over.

I finally admit that these episodes have terrorized me for close to a decade. Still, my trip to see the psychiatrist is not without hurdles. Even as I drive to the appointment to ask if there's something wrong with my brain, I keep thinking that I don't really need to go. *I could stop the car, turn around and head home. I could.*

Thankfully, I don't. A wiser self wrests control of the situation, demanding I continue toward my destination, while seizing the opportunity to remind me of past episodes that have broken my defences and humbled me sufficiently *not* to pretend that everything is fine. But on this particular day in August 2011, everything *is* fine.

Here I am: sixty-three years old, tanned and fit, enjoying a powerful surge of real estate deals after taking most of the summer off. *Summertime and the livin' is easy,* which is why I flirt with the idea of bailing on the appointment. Fortunately, I know the truth about the two faces of Patricia. It is time to come out of hiding.

ONCE I AM in the psychiatrist's office, I tell him pointblank that I want to be *in the system*—the mental health system—just to be on the safe side. I also tell him that I am ready to hear the truth about what I am dealing with: whether it's real or not. I'm here for answers. Still, I bite back the urge to warn, *All that glitters is not gold,* or cite a rhyme that comes to mind, but I don't. The words rattle in my head nonetheless.

> *There was a little girl,*
> *And she had a little curl*
> *Right in the middle of her forehead.*
> *When she was good*
> *She was very, very good,*
> *And when she was bad she was horrid.*

I like the psychiatrist immediately, particularly his calm style. But before he begins the intake interview, I disclose what I feel is essential information. I explain that when I'm in the grip of an episode, the *bad* part of me cannot imagine the *good* part of me, or that it ever exists. And vice versa. There is no crossover or connection between the two. It is as if these parts occupy different, locked compartments of my brain, the experiences of *good* or *bad* so deeply ingrained and convincing that neither side remembers a diametrically different self.

He nods slightly. "Take me back to when this all started."

My answer is immediate. "The year is 2000, the turn of the century."

"What happens in 2000?"

THE YEAR 2000 is a time of overwhelming change for me. On a research scale that measures life stressors, I am right up there—probably over the top. My divorce is done; I am a single mother of an eleven-year-old daughter; I celebrate New Year's 2000 by taking back my family name. In the spring I buy a beautiful old waterfront property that costs double what I can afford, with another house still to sell.

Through grace and grit, when it's time to pay for the property I bring in a partner to share the financial load of the purchase. It looks like a stroke of genius—perhaps it is—but the process costs me dearly. I lose not only ten pounds I cannot afford to lose but also the ability to recognize the wreck I have become. On the day a friend helps me move into my new house, I drag my dead-weight body around, opening a few boxes, spaced out and lethargic. Within a few hours I crawl into bed and stay there for three days, curled in a tight fetal position: teeth clattering, unable to eat or speak, cold and shaking, buried under a down quilt, my arms binding my body as if to keep myself in one piece. Throughout this time my friend continues to unpack and quietly set up my house.

What I remember about summer 2000 is sitting in a pink chair in a black fog, day after day looking out over the ocean—my mind dull and listless, devoid of thought, feeling, or affect. My greatest challenge is to leave my house to buy food and force myself to eat. I thank God Sarah is away at camp for the summer. Occasionally, I write her a card and drop it in the mailbox, knowing it will reach her somewhere along a wilderness route near Canoe Lake in Algonquin Park, Ontario. Occasionally, I notice myself wearing my Lululemon pants inside out. One day I venture out in two different shoes. Polishing my nails is out of the question. Other than writing cards for Sarah, I am too shaky to do much of anything.

AS I TELL my story I become aware that I am draining it of all emotion—rendering the account flat and lifeless, like siphoning blood from a body. But the real story sounds like this.

Like Queen Inanna in the Sumerian myth of her descent to the underworld, where she hangs on a meat hook—bloodied and dying—moaning, "I suffer, I suffer, I suffer," I hear my own muffled voice in the thundering din of an approaching storm. *Too much, too much, too much.*

FALL 2000 GOES from bad to worse. While I cannot explain what is happening to me, I can paint a picture. The flat affect of summer mutates into a high-strung anxiety that hounds me day and night—especially night—when I lie in bed praying for sleep, my mind wrecked and obsessing about nothing in particular, my body shot with a chemical rush not unlike what I imagine people would feel if they took crystal meth.

Sleep is ragged at best. Any thought of relief from my mind as I climb into bed is destroyed during the night. Panic jolts me awake repeatedly, leaving me lying there, terrified and sweating in soaked sheets. I try it all: St. John's wort, melatonin—first one milligram, then two, and finally three—before pitching them aside and giving up on that remedy as well. I try an over-the-counter blue gelcap bullet called Sleep-eze, which helps *sometimes, somewhat.* My sister, Joann, tells me that Sleep-eze is bad for my liver, but it's not my liver I'm worried about. Sometimes I think the best thing I could do would be to slug myself over the head with a hammer and put myself out of my misery.

September through December 2000 I wake up each morning with a feeling of dread, which is driven not only by jarring sleep that wipes out my energy but also by the lack of meaning of my existence. During the day I haul myself around feeling wired and tired, but more often feeling wired and deranged. Jittery and tremulous, I ride a crazed beast, a horse with no name.

January 2, 2001, the morning after what feels like an endless holiday season, I implode. I drop into a nearby chair and collapse, which is when a thought forms in my mind that I have never before considered. But I hear it— clear and uncomplicated—arising of its own accord. *I need help. I can't live like this.*

I can't remember how I get there. Maybe I crawl to my neighbour's house. But I reach the door and walk in, half-fall into the arms of Mary, the eighty-six-year-old lady who leads me to her sofa, where I lie curled in a tight ball. She might be old but she is smart. *Crisis here!* is her take on the situation, and she is correct. Within seconds she is on the phone, wedging me into an appointment with her own doctor that very day. I remain on her sofa wrapped in a mohair blanket, unable to talk, my body lurching in strange spasms until Joann arrives to collect me. I am a quivering mess.

The doctor takes one look at me and reaches for his prescription pad. I ask no questions; he offers no explanations, which is just as well. I could not process them anyway. I am too far gone to care about giving a name to what is wrong with me. Any sense of competency or volition I might have had—even knowing who I am—is wiped away. My desperation pitches me to an unbearable place. I have no pride; I only want relief.

I grab the prescription like a child grabbing candy and Joann leads me out of the office to the pharmacy next door to have it filled. I celebrate New Year's 2001 by starting drugs.

I FINISH THIS segment of my story with what I consider an important distinction.

This lack of competency, or volition, that I am talking about is *not* a question of self-esteem or confidence. It is a question of Self. I am No-Self. Self is gone.

The psychiatrist, listening intently although not saying a lot, gets the picture. "The depressed brain on an MRI looks different—dark and dull—whereas a healthy brain lights up with colour," he tells me.

In a simple statement he uses a word that makes me crawl with shame. But when he says the word *depressed*, I can accept it.

He continues. "This is biology we're talking about. An illness in the brain, no different than any other illness. It needs to be treated."

I listen.

"How many episodes have you had?" he asks.

"Probably five or six, over the past ten or eleven years."

"What are you like when you're feeling good?" His genuine question prompts a straightforward answer.

"Very good," I reply quietly. "The complete opposite of when I'm horrid." The words roll out easily. "Clear-thinking, passionate; creative, intuitive; sometimes smart, often exuberant." I pause before adding a final note. "All the things *I'm not* when I'm horrid. When I'm good, my world is words, joy, energy, beauty."

Our sixty minutes are up. We agree that I do not need a new prescription at this time, nor do I want one. But I have found what I do need: a man whom I can trust and, after all these years, an answer to my question in one beautiful word: *biology*. I leave the appointment feeling something I rarely feel as I ride roughshod over myself: a hint of compassion and a glimmer of gentleness toward myself.

We have covered a large expanse of personal history in one small room, but the story requires more depth and detail. In the ten years between January 2001 when I start taking drugs and August 2011 when I am driving to meet the psychiatrist, I swing between *normal* and *not normal*; alternate between taking drugs and taking myself off them, hanging on to the remote hope of setting my life on a firm foundation.

Throughout these years—whether the good or the bad years—I constantly seek therapies, because I am a seeker and because I long for comfort from the roller coaster I call my life, with its exhilarating highs and deadly lows. For these reasons, I dabble in a dizzying array of treatments: meditation, neural linguistic programming, ecstatic postures, hypnosis, past-life regression, aromatherapy, emotional freedom technique, cranial sacral, therapeutic acupuncture, cleanses, and colonics. Still, I harbour a distrust that any of these therapies can help.

DURING THIS TIME my life careens along an unpredictable course. But despite the emotional extremes, I carry on. Doing what I do. During the normal times, I run on my own high spirits, setting goals that capture my imagination and accomplishing some of my proudest achievements. I go back to university, join Toastmasters International, and publish a memoir.

Prompted by a dream in which an arrogant professor challenges me in front of a group of students—*If you think you are so smart, maybe you should get a master's degree*—I switch careers mid-life, returning my real estate licence and enrolling in a master's programme in counselling. By the time I earn my degree, I receive the best gift I can imagine for my fiftieth birthday.

When I begin writing poetry at the age of eight, I intuitively recognize the power of words. Even then they enchanted me. Decades later a friend invites me as a guest to Morningstars Toastmasters, the local club of the international organization, which claims me as one of its own. Likewise, I find a place to express my love of language, including its nerdy cousin, grammar. Seven years after joining the club I sport the coveted Distinguished Toastmaster badge.

During this same time I fulfill a lifelong dream and publish the memoir. With newfound knowledge from my master's work, I discover a deeper understanding of what our culture casually calls "life transitions," which are in fact often periods of devastating change. In a moment of insight while mowing the lawn one spring morning, I grasp the meaning of these changes by placing them within the ancient concept of initiation. This sudden shift in language creates a similar shift in perception—bringing understanding and dignity to individuals enduring some of life's toughest times, including me. The book becomes my sixtieth birthday gift to myself.

My successes during these high-functioning periods stand in startling contrast to the debilitating moods of the *not normal* times that inevitably follow.

AS I LOOK back to my mid-thirties, I see the allure of clothes, career, lifestyle, and lovers begins to fade. My attention turns inward to the study of psychology, Jungian therapy, dreams, spirituality, introspection, and the need to take an honest inventory of what looks like a glamorous life. I thirst for new knowledge and delve into this inner work as if my life depends on it. Journalling becomes my refuge, providing the security I need to descend to the nether regions of my psyche— echoing a theme found in the Greek myth of Ariadne and the labyrinth.

In the myth Ariadne assists Theseus in his descent to the underworld by offering him a silk cord, which he uses to find his way out of the labyrinth. My journal entries serve the same purpose. Often it is only the spider-silk tethers trailing behind each word like a safety cord that allow me to descend and trust that I can return to solid ground.

AS I LOOK back specifically to the journals written since the year 2001, I draw a timeline, marking periods of abundant energy and well-being with a fluorescent yellow highlighter and marking the flat, deadening times with a thick black line. I begin to sniff out a pattern, which looks roughly like one good year followed by a bad year—after which I return to my doctor and return to my drugs. The exercise of charting my emotional states with contrasting colours shines a light on vital information. I can see clearly now how the pattern repeats.

On–off, on–off. When my brain burns hot and fast and floods me with fiery energy, I run on my own high-octane fuel and get by without drugs. But after periods of exceptional activity and productivity, I crash and burn like Icarus who soars too high, flies too close to the sun, and plunges to his death.

My falls from grace build slowly but with telltale signs: overstimulation and an obsessive mind. Most insidious of all is the relentless insomnia, which plagues me month after month—breaking my spirit and leaving me frantic. Such is the toxic mix that takes me to the tipping point. *Too much, too much, too much.*

I begin to speculate that the brain possesses a self-regulating system that calls a time-out, which forces a stop order from the driving pressure to perform and shine. I imagine the mechanism kicking in before the brain short circuits and incinerates. To validate my hunch, I turn to the journals to remember the periods when I call this time-out and implode into myself. Rough written passages and primitive drawings force me to confront my desperate stabs to make sense of what is happening. I discover entries that capture the bedlam in my mind.

First journal entry:

*So fucking tired of this bullshit. Waking up at 4 am, crazed
in my own body. Brain crawling with chemicals.*

*What is me? What is my body? Is this scrawny version
the new me—or will it return to its former self? Is this caterpillar me? Attacking the emerging cells of the butterfly
forming inside the cocoon? Arms clutching body, seeking
solace under a wet blanket.*

*I do not recognize this self. It is foreign. I fight it. Old
systems break down.*

*Is this my soul calling me? Wake Up! Wake Up! Come
talk to me of your grief, your despair, your longing, and yes,
your creeping suspicion that you will remain in this madness
forever. Wake Up! Sharpen your pencil and talk to me.*

Second entry:

*Nothing left inside. Drained of all life. Crawl back to bed
on a sunny morning. Accounts overdraw, cheques bounce,
everything slides.*

*Force myself to make calls to stop further damage. The
structure of my life in shambles.*

Me? Disappeared.

Third entry:

*Scratch my head with long red nails. Blood gucks up the
hair. Scabs form. Pick scabs—again and again—make
scabs bleed—again and again. Red blood on white Kleenex.*

No more looking good. Mom always looked good. What a death-box her life must have been.

A sarcastic voice: Ready to go back to work?

No!

Why not?

Technology terrors, need to produce. Feigning interest, drawing from an empty well.

Look at these toenails. Disgusting, chipped, pathetic, a new low in personal care.

A dream called "Death Knell" declares: the form is finished.

Fussed about whether my graphic artist knows how to design a book. Buried in my brain, my own cuckoo's nest.

The form is finished. God. Release me from this manic mind or take me home.

After the journals I turn to a sketch book, which I resort to when words fail. Feelings too ugly to utter, I draw my anguish instead.

First image:

Drag wire brush over my body. Lacerate skin. Bloody striations the only escape for beleaguered spirit. Black and blue and red all over.

Second image:

Red jagged lines instead of words. Wolf claws at brain. Red of eyes and fangs and blood. Brain devoured.

Third image:

Body lies on bed of nails. Bound in black barbed wire. Face, contorted blue. Electric shocks jolt my brain. Trapped in a vortex, cannot move. Appalling pain, the mind succumbs.

For all the beauty of my home, Rose Pointe Ocean House, I often live in hell. Like a force of nature, an episode leaves the body battered, the spirit beaten. The hope of returning to normal destroyed in the process.

There is no morning after.

THROUGHOUT THE TEN years between 2001 and 2011, Paxil is my prince and drug of choice. And although I am inconstant in my affection toward him—turning to him only for temporary comfort and then dropping him—ultimately, it is Paxil who dumps me in the spring of 2011. Without warning, my prince becomes indifferent to my needs and abandons me with brutal finality.

In the aftermath of Paxil and in consultation with my family doctor, I try four different drugs and combinations thereof in two short months, all with terrifying results. Finally, I declare, "Doctors don't know," and take myself off all drugs, cold turkey. I determine to ride it out alone, still not knowing the name of what I suffer from, but choosing denial over the alternative of living within the rigid confines of psychiatric labels, which feel as appealing as a coffin.

Miraculously, I discover an antidote for *too much* encoded in a single word: *no.* With surprising ease, I push back at the world that is too much with me and edit my life with unhesitating strokes. I remove myself from the schedule at my sister's store; remove myself from floor duty at my office; turn over deals for associates to complete; shut off my pager and shut off my computer, except for those times, usually late on a Friday afternoon, when I turn it on to delete hundreds of emails accumulated over the week. "Are you sure you want to permanently delete the selected messages?" it asks. Without missing a beat I hit "Yes" and feel instant gratification verging on giddiness. I stop short of posting a sign at my back door, declaring *CLOSED to all but me.*

In the process of tuning in and dropping out, I recover my all-but-forgotten sensuous self as I grant myself a holiday in my own home on the ocean. I respond to nothing but my own impulses: my need for food, exercise, or sleep; the call of the ocean, wind, and weather. An added blessing: my mind takes a holiday as well.

The months of June through August 2011, I swim in the ocean daily, ignoring the relentlessly cold temperature of the water. Early mornings when the tide is high, I slip out of my deck chair, drop my light cotton robe, and slide naked into the salt water. I commit to a rigorous food plan, eliminate all wine and liquor from my diet, paddle my kayak, smell my roses, tend my garden, and revel in simple pleasures like hanging my cottons outside on the line to dry and, in a more discreet fashion, hanging my black lace underwear on the covered porch to dry, watching it flutter in the summer wind like Tibetan prayer flags.

I follow the progression of the sun throughout the day, carrying my books and moving from one pink chair to the next to catch the final rays of afternoon sun. I find books that fill me with gratitude for solitude and silence. *Gift from the Sea* by Anne Morrow Lindbergh, *A Year by the Sea* and *A Walk on the Beach* by Joan Anderson, and Angela Thirkell's *August Folly*, the inspiration for my annual garden party.

BY THE END of August 2011, when I am driving to my appointment with the psychiatrist for the specific purpose of securing a foothold in the mental health system, I have regained a gentle humour, my joy for life, and feel strong, upbeat, and healthy.

AFTER THE IDYLLS of summer and the golden flush of well-being, September 2011 strikes with a vengeance. My computer crashes; a new leadership role I've taken on in Toastmasters International begins full bore. Overwhelmed by extra responsibility, I'm sidelined—left standing in the dust—my horror heightened by the doom of fall, returning sleeplessness, and obsessive thoughts that reach a new frenzy. *I am in trouble.*

Like my computer, I crash in short order, witnessing myself in a full-blown panic in London Drugs as I struggle over the purchase of olive oil, canned salmon, toilet paper, and paper towels. By early October I hit the tipping point. Failing to use the word *crisis* when I book an appointment with the psychiatrist's nurse the following morning, I wait an unbearable two months before seeing him, during which time I enter a morbid phase I call "defaulting to death." Death is everywhere.

After a second sleepless night of reading *Still Alice* by Lisa Genova, my hands burned into the book and unable to put it down, my mind is twisted into the belief that, like the woman in the story, a brilliant Harvard neuroscientist, I suffer from early Alzheimer's. I rise before dawn to rid myself of the horror that has haunted me for the past forty-eight hours. Book in hand—brain on fire—I walk to the front of my lawn at the edge of the ocean, howling like a banshee, "I hate this fucking book!" and hurl it into the ocean. It disappears in a flash, like I could too, if I would just walk into the ocean, letting my flirty, new black-and-white rubber boots fill with water and drag me down like Virginia Woolf, with the rocks in her pockets transporting her to the death I imagine.

By early November, when I am finally back in the psychiatrist's office, he could rightly ask, "Who is this woman?" who bears no resemblance to the woman he met in August. Cold and shivering, I huddle in his chair, feeling like a fool in my shiny, new golden raincoat. I'm thankful he's smart enough to spare the talk and write out two new prescriptions instead. Ultimately, my returning health is due as much to his manner as his medication. I need his intelligence, integrity, and authority in order to begin the healing process.

But four days later, with the prescriptions still stuffed in my bag, I remain anxious about the idea of going back on drugs. The thought of taking them indefinitely, as the psychiatrist has alluded, feels pathetic. Yet here I am, sitting in my shiny, new silver Mercedes in the parking lot outside the pharmacy—jittery and tremulous—confused and afraid to walk into the clinic to have my prescriptions filled, despite having just driven into a concrete barricade.

If that isn't pathetic, I don't know what is.

This clinches the deal. I grab my bag, open the car door, lock up, and stride into the pharmacy.

ON THE ROAD I have travelled since 2001 seeking a more balanced state of mind, I can finally declare that since 2011 I have successfully stayed on the same drugs for more than six years. I now consider myself—more or less—cured of my ambivalence about taking them. I am watchful, but no longer wary. Watchful of the progressive slide into an all-too-familiar episode marked by feelings of inundation and hopelessness. Through trial by fire I have learned to cut, delete, say, "No."

After reading *An Unquiet Mind: A Memoir of Moods and Madness* by Kay Redfield Jamison, I have gained a new understanding of my experiences. I recognize that the passion, imagination, and spirit of one part of me is directly related to the desperation and deadliness of the other. The *normal* and the *not normal* inform and infuse each other.

I reflect on the word *resilience*, which is often used to describe the human spirit, but I believe that another word cuts closer to the truth, drives deeper into the depths. The word is *resurrection*. None other captures the *death that is real* nor the *return that is miraculous*.

I REALIZE THAT it is no accident that I am writing this story during the height of summer, when I reach my perfect pitch of joy. And likewise, I know that it would have been ludicrous to have tackled this topic at any other time during the past sixteen years. But today I do not have to be hauled out of hiding to come clean. Still, it takes the intervention of a trickster to catch me red-handed and set the matter straight, once and for all.

Recently, I catch the ferry into Vancouver to donate blood at the Canadian Blood Services clinic. After completing the questionnaire to determine if I am fit to donate, an efficient young nurse, who is already reading my form as she walks in front of me, ushers me into a screened cubicle next to the waiting area. By the time I am seated on the hard, moulded chair, she queries me on an item that has caught her eye, a tiny blackened-out box that declares "Yes" to the question: *In the last three days have you taken any medicine or drugs [pills including Aspirin or shots], other than birth control pills and vitamins?*

She asks in a loud, superior tone, "What is the name of the drug you have taken?"

"Drugs," I reply curtly.

"Well, what are the names of the *drugs* you have taken?"

This is not going well. "Actually," I reply, "I don't remember the names." However, I see no alternative but to comply with her suggestion. I take my cell phone, place a call to my local pharmacy, and ask for the names of my prescriptions, waiting impatiently and feeling naked in front of the other donors who have no doubt heard our exchange. Finally, I have my answers, which I deliver to her. Snooty and to the point.

"Escitalopram. For anxiety. Clonazepam. For sleeping."

She asks no further questions, and I am considered acceptable, although I feel shaken and irritated. A magnanimous impulse to donate blood forces me to publicly face an irrefutable reality. Call it what I will. I deal with mental health issues.

8

THE

FIRE

WINTER MORNINGS BEGIN early in our house on the hill in Smithers, British Columbia, with our father, Jack, already up and working outside by the time my sister, Joann, and I rouse ourselves from sleep. While we stay tucked in bed, toasty from nights under quilts and Hudson's Bay blankets, he blows snow with his new machine and hauls wood into the house for the fireplace. Maybe even feels a tingle of pleasure in his outside work; maybe even whistles softly to himself, despite the frigid temperatures. Watching from the warmth of our bedroom, there is magic in seeing the glorious, white plumes of snowy feathers issue from the blower, like outstretched wings of a giant egret, but the chores concerning snow, wood, and fires hold none of the same charm or beauty.

Once Joann and I leave home for university we visit Smithers less often than we could, but when we return it is clear that wood remains a dominant element of family life.

A stockpile of firewood flanking the driveway grows each year, becoming a fortress against the ills that might befall a family. The sight of Jack's massive wall closing in the property becomes the bane of our mother's existence. She is not a woman to be fenced in, yet it is not until after she dies, when the tall stand of cedars backing the wall has also died as a result of the woodpile blocking their roots and cutting off their water supply, that Jack decides to cut down her beloved trees and dismantle the colossal wood-pile. *Too little, too late.* It is one of our father's regrets that he did not move the pile earlier.

GROWING UP IN Smithers teaches me a fundamental life lesson. A man's work is outside; a woman's work, inside. The idea of my mother blowing snow, hauling wood, or building fires is as inconceivable as my father wearing an apron and making gravy in the kitchen. Still, with no son to carry on the family gene for tending fires and me being the only one of two sisters to own houses with wood-burning fireplaces, the need to watch over fires falls on me by default. When Jack dies three years after our mother, Joann and I sell the family home in Smithers. I claim the one thing that I want shipped back to my house in Gibsons: a commercial-sized baker's flour bin filled with fragrant, dry fir kindling, split and stored by Jack himself. This is the gift I choose, and I handle each stick of kindling like the gold that it is for starting fires.

In the year 2000 I celebrate the dawn of the new century by reverting to my family name after my divorce;

selling the home I lived in with my ex-husband, Brian, and daughter, Sarah; and buying a one-hundred-year-old waterfront home that I can barely afford. In the years between 2000 and 2014—with no partner in my life or lover in my bed—I shoulder the care of the grand old home and property myself: patching wooden shakes, caulking single-pane windows, trapping rodents and evicting raccoons and sea otters squatting under the house with their young. I spend countless hours feeding fires with their insatiable appetite for seasoned wood, as well as mowing lawns, weeding gardens growing out of control, and pruning fruit trees and shrubs. I do it all—both the man's outside work and the woman's inside work—and I do it with the same satisfaction I imagine our father felt when I watched him as a young girl from our bedroom in Smithers, at work outside on minus-twenty-degree mornings.

By the fall of 2014 events conspire to change my outlook and bring me to my knees. After years of coaxing fires in the old stone fireplace, the wood bin in the garage is close to empty. Between November and December, while I wait for the delivery of what Bill, the handyman, promises is a load of beautiful kindling and dry wood, my spirit starts to buckle. Four interminable weeks of being stood up, with no sign of Bill or the delivery truck that he hopes to borrow from a friend, take their toll and send me into a tailspin beyond reason. I am a woman scorned, and spooked as well by the strange mood I can't seem to shake. I tell myself that this quest for firewood is overheated to the extreme, but my mind spikes with anxiety nonetheless. *I am floundering and I know it.*

With the saga of the missing wood overshadowing my thoughts, I feel an unusual bitterness rising in me, caught as I am in conflicting feelings that relate to a young girl's notion of a man's work and a woman's work. I hear myself protest, *What am I? A pioneer?* The truth is that I am sick and tired of doing it all, but deeper still—below the disappointment that has settled on my life like a pall—lurks a feeling of abandonment. The role of fire keeper passed to me through my father's lineage becomes a source of smouldering resentment.

As Christmas bears down on me with no firewood in sight and exactly one week to go before I make my classic Christmas Eve chowder, I concede defeat and send an email to my guests coming to dinner. The subject sets the stage for revised expectations.

Subject: Fire's (not) Burning

Good morning friends and family—a Christmas note on a cold morning. At this time in the season, the ideal of *fire's burning, fire's burning* might be just that: an ideal. The truth is that I have no firewood and no way to create the roaring fire that we have come to love in my home. My efforts to find wood have been squelched and thrown me into a turmoil about what a home should be—comforting, beautiful, and welcoming—not unlike what a woman should be.

Knowing I won't be building you a fire on Christmas Eve
makes me feel bleak and sad. But I have decided that, if I
must, I will light up the home with candles instead. It will
be—*whatever* it will be—but please do not ask why we
have no fire.

I want to share my feelings so you understand my sensi-
tivity about this matter. Love P.

Within minutes of receiving my message, Joann is
on the phone expressing concern and solutions. "I'm
going to phone Colin," she states directly, talking about
the man who was my partner between 1997 and 1999,
after Brian and I divorced. Joann's reason for reaching out to Colin makes sense. She knows the story of
Christmas Eve, 1997, when I asked Colin if he would
agree to Sarah, Brian, and my spending some private
time together as a family on Christmas Day, when what
appeared to be an irreparable rift erupted between Colin
and me in response to my request.

· Late in the afternoon on Christmas Eve back in 1997,
disaster looms. Heartsick and torn between old and new
loyalties, I am upstairs in the kitchen when the doorbell
rings and Colin and Sarah dash downstairs to greet someone at the door. I hear a second man's voice, loud noises
from the carport, and shortly after, a truck driving away.
Moments later I recognize a familiar sound from years
ago—the sound of my father stacking wood in Smithers
back in the fifties: *clunk, clunk, clunk*.

But on this December day in 1997 it is Colin who places his hurt aside, takes charge, and restocks our meagre pile. I hear them—this man and my young daughter working outside together—engrossed in stacking the wood that will fuel our fires for the winter months. My eyes blur with tears as I continue preparing dinner: peeling, chopping, whisking, stirring. Sarah and I will have a Christmas after all and Colin will be at our table for dinner. His gift—plain and simple—speaks louder than luxury items because it is not glamour I long for, but something older and deeper. Like my father, Colin's instinct tells him that it is natural for a man to provide and care for a woman.

I understand why Joann turns to Colin for help, but my response to her suggestion is alarm: why would she ask Colin to help me after all these years? I feel vulnerable, having to ask an old friend for help. But when she hears my resistance to her idea, she admits that she has already called him and, yes, he has agreed to find me some firewood before Christmas. He phones me shortly after to confirm his promise, and I know he is good for it. I can expect him on the twenty-fourth of December, precisely seventeen years to the day that he ordered a load of wood to be delivered to our house, which he stacked with Sarah while I prepared Christmas chowder in the kitchen upstairs, doubting that our relationship would survive the shambles I created.

Now seventeen years later, on this same December day in 2014, Sarah and I are living in the old sprawling home on the ocean. When Colin arrives midday with a small load of wood, once again I am preparing the same seafood dinner that I made in 1997. Through the darkening afternoon, he works in the freezing garage with an ax and chopping block, splitting the logs into the specific size I need for my fireplace. It is black outside by the time he knocks at the door, announcing he has finished his job. As he turns to leave, he hesitates and asks sheepishly if I want him to light my fire.

"No thanks," I laugh. "I've got everything I need." I reach out to give him a quick hug and he's gone. It is only now that I feel the bone-aching weariness I have struggled with for weeks that I realize I am sick and tired in the truest sense. I have run out of steam.

My lively group of guests arrives at six o'clock in the evening. Snow clinging to their clothes, they bring brisk winter air into the house with them. The festive table is set; dinner is ready to serve. The fire burns vigorously and the smell of cedar boughs warms the room. All is ready but me: I am wearing pyjamas and a tacky old robe—too exhausted to put on the new Christmas dress I planned to wear—but still wanting to pour my guests a glass of champagne and wish them Merry Christmas.

After serving the champagne I slip away from the party, heading to my bedroom. I climb gratefully into bed and leave them enjoying a cozy winter's night. Throughout the evening I move in and out of a feverish sleep. Wrapped in my down quilt, I hear sounds of conversation in the background, the snap of fire, and eventually—as my guests clean up like Christmas elves and leave the house spotless—the tinkle of breaking glass and stifled laughter. I picture it all in the comfort of the moment.

Fire's burning, fire's burning
Draw nearer.

9

THE

PIE

HE'S GOT TWO weeks. Even so, when my sister, Joann, meets me at the Calgary airport, she says it's too late for me to see our father tonight. He still goes to bed early and is no doubt already in a fitful sleep, which has been his pattern and plague as long as I can remember. Working his entire adult life on the Canadian National Railway in Smithers, British Columbia, he's been put at odds with half the world by the irregular hours, which raised hell with his sleep. She tells me she's given him her bedroom. Seems to think nothing of turning over her big master suite and indeed her sanctuary on the top floor, the whole setup larger and more luxurious than he's ever had.

The room sits high in the house, with windows thrown open to a view of the garden below. A warm August wind whistles through the poplars, yet the Elbow River bordering the property hardly makes a sound, what with the summer dry spell. The river now meanders lazy and slow rather than rushing to unknown destinations. A king-size pine bed with corner posts and a tufted headboard brought back from California dominates the room. All of it as comforting as the quilt and bleached cotton duvet covering the bed. Joann tells me he spends most of his time in the room. I imagine him sitting up in the bed, leaning against the soft headboard.

"Reading?" I ask.

"No, his eyes are too bad. That damn glaucoma should have been caught years ago by his doctor, but it wasn't. No," she says. "He mainly listens to baseball on the radio, hanging on to every word, especially when the Jays are playing. Thank God they're on a winning streak to the World Series."

A flash of anger spikes my response. "Well, if you ask me, I'd say it was criminal how no one bothered to encourage him to accept an offer—right out of high school—to play for a professional farm team."

Joann softens the outburst. "It was the Depression and times were tough. Besides, he couldn't bear the guilt of leaving his mother with three younger children.

"At least he's got his baseball," she continues, "which is pretty much his entertainment these days. And I laugh when I hear him upstairs—cheering and calling out plays from the bed. It's good for both of us," she says, smiling and reaching out to hug me. "Time for bed."

I nod, set my indignation aside, and hold her tight. "Good night, my dear, and thanks for being an amazing caregiver."

The next morning I find Joann busy in the kitchen wearing a blue silk robe from Bali and chopping a mound of greens and grasses and something I don't recognize.

"Hey you!" she turns and grins, commenting as she sees me already dressed in my standard black capris, faded tank top, and sandals. "Glad to see you're ready for the day."

"What's this?" I ask, pointing to the growing heap on the counter. Taking the lid off a pot simmering on the stove and peering into the frothing water, I press for answers. "And what's in here?"

She laughs. "Corn silk, horsetail, and potato skins— for a potion I'm brewing for Dad—a recipe from Gonzalo and an ancient Peruvian remedy supposedly good for the bladder." She elaborates. "Dad's doctor tells us it's lymphoma, but he also says that he will die of bladder failure before he dies of cancer. When I heard that I decided to contact Gonzalo, and this is his concoction. I boil up a batch every week. I tell Dad it's Inca tea."

"Dad doesn't mind?" I ask, voicing my suspicions.

She's quick to his defence. "Dad's pretty mellow these days and less ornery. His old habit of rejecting anything out of the ordinary seems to have disappeared. And his harsh style? That's softened too." She chuckles. "Well, somewhat."

I push for more details. "So he drinks his tea with good humour?"

"Yup," she comes back. "Says he likes the sound of an ancient remedy; says it might just help that tired old body of his. He calls me his nurse and seems to like that, too.

At least he knows he's loved, and he trusts me. In the end that's all that matters. He's refused all medication so there's just my magic brew and the occasional special brownie."

"*Special brownie?* What does he think of that?"

"He thinks it helps him relax at night; settles his nerves for a better sleep." She recalls, "Once he asked, 'What's in this thing?' I told him, 'Nothing that can hurt you,' and that put an end to his question. He's happy enough with an evening treat now and then."

We're quiet for a moment, as I digest the information.

"Good," I reply slowly, holding up a thin sheaf of paper. "Then maybe he'll be okay with a story I've written for him. I think I'll go see him now, while he's resting."

I approach the sofa where he lies and place a low wooden stool that I find in the kitchen next to it, drop my body onto the stool and settle into a seated squat. Elbows propped on thighs, arms outstretched toward him, and hands holding the paper. A few inches closer and I could touch him, but I don't. He lies in corpse pose—legs stretched the length of the sofa, arms by his side. An airline-issue, black satin Zorro mask covers his eyes, secured with skinny strips of elastic wrapped around his ears.

I speak softly, "Good morning, Dad. How are you?"

I venture into murky waters. "I have something for you. I've written a story that I'd like to read. I call it 'Jack.' It's about you. Would that be fine?"

He clears his throat but makes no comment. I take the sound to mean "Yes." The silence urges me forward; if he didn't want me to continue, he would have stopped me dead in my tracks. I begin reading.

Jack's father returns from World War I with a badly shot-up leg. Not long after, a surgeon's knife slices the leg off—above the knee—to stop gangrene from ravaging what's left of it. The twelve-year-old boy struggles to make sense of what's happening, but no one speaks. A shroud of silence descends on the house. Others' words seep in through invisible cracks—boys his own age and well-meaning folk from the northern town—their voices hushed with sympathy and horror.

What a tragedy, the father such a fine athlete and a competitive runner at that.

So young and now with no leg.

What will he do?

And the family, how will they survive?

No one seems to know. Maybe he can get a job through his grandfather at the bank.

Each whisper drives shame into Jack's body. Two images do battle in his mind. One glorious—his father winning a race. The other grotesque—the missing leg. And then the most grotesque of all. His father in the backseat of a car. Dead. Wrists slit; blackened blood ruining the seat. Suicide. For the father, perhaps an end to his grief. For the son, the beginning.

I stop reading; look at him closely. He's much thinner now—the flesh disappearing along with the brusque manner.

Finally, he speaks. "Some of it . . . you didn't get quite right."

Coming from him I know the absence of sharper words signals high praise. I agree. "You're right. Joann and I never heard the full story, and I had to piece it together the best I could."

Stillness settles around us, reassures me that connection has been offered, perhaps even received. The occasion requires nothing more.

Minutes pass, and what follows makes no sense, nor can I imagine how an idea can take hold so quickly. Still, I follow the impulse and ease into the *temenos* without pausing to think. "Dad," I ask, "do you mind if I file your nails?"

He responds with the same indifference he did to my earlier request: with silence, which I take as permission granted. I rise from my seated squat, stand upright, and leave his side to find my emery board. When I return, he is still lying in corpse pose, still wearing the black Zorro mask. I approach carefully.

"Dad," I begin, "if you could just slide over a bit I could sit on the edge of the sofa. That would make it easier for me to file your nails."

He shifts into the back cushions, allowing me to claim a tentative hold on the skinny edge of the sofa. I begin with his right hand, which is closest to me, and then with his left, which takes some manoeuvring to find the right angle for filing.

Dad once had stunning good looks, which I remember from a photograph taken in his mid-twenties. Dressed in a baseball uniform and cleats, his left hand in a glove and right arm thrust back to throw a ball, Jack is a younger man by half a century. In this golden moment, he is a picture of youth and vigor: tall and slim, wavy brown hair, glorious smile, and perfectly even teeth.

Today, only his hands defy his age. They remain straight and strong, still without age spots, still with the unusually large, flat nail beds I inherit from him. He allows my curious ministrations and in so doing grants us an intimacy we have never known. Or perhaps an intimacy that is only possible due to the certainty of his death. Instinctively, I tuck the feeling of this time together into my heart—where it endures as a gift of grace.

I finish with a simple remark, "Okay, Dad, I'm done. I'll leave you to rest now."

"Thanks, kid," he replies with unexpected warmth. Unexpected, because I'd heard him call Joann and my friends "kid" when we were growing up—a sign of his affection. But he never said that to me.

"You're welcome, Dad!" Then dropping my voice like a co-conspirator I add, "Besides, I have something else to do,"—dragging out the suspense for an important announcement. "I have a pie to make—Mom's lemon meringue pie. I brought the recipe with me."

"Good," he says.

I LEAVE HIS side and head into the kitchen, calling over my shoulder as I go, "I'd better get started or we won't be ready for afternoon tea." With our brief exchange, the air around us lightens, brightens.

Joann stands at the kitchen sink, gazing out to the river. "Look at this," I say, nudging into her musings as I hand her Mom's recipe: eons old, splattered with ingredients of all sorts, and faded to be barely legible. But it is remarkable nonetheless, because this is Mom's handwriting, which maintained its classic form throughout her life, even when she was dying. Even when she wrote goodbye to more than one hundred people with personalized letters sent via Canada Post.

At the time I receive what will become her last letter, I ponder her unusual choice of paper, with roadrunners from winters in Arizona, pastoral scenes, floral bouquets, and finally, yellow lined foolscap. But it is not until after she dies that I realize she depleted her matching paper. At the end she was down to the last dregs of her stock.

Joann looks intently at the recipe. "My God it's *her.* And *that* is her beautiful writing."

"Wait," I continue, the excitement of another surprise punctuating my words. "Look at this!" I cry, handing her a second sheet of paper. We peer at a certificate dated 1935 that reads *The MacLean Method of Writing: Advanced Certificate*, which bears our mother's name: Antoinette Emily Bourgon. She is eighteen years old and attending Normal School for teacher training in Victoria, British Columbia. Even a tiny black-and-white photograph taken at the same time captures her exotic beauty, with its hints of Sophia Loren—although not as outrageously sexy—but gorgeous and wholesome. The narrow confines of the photograph's square white border barely contain her high energy as she strides along the sidewalk in front of the Empress Hotel in a fitted black winter coat with a natural fox fur collar.

I turn my attention back to Joann. "Time to get cooking. Will you help?" I ask, knowing our production will go smoother with my sister in her own kitchen.

"Sure," she says easily. "Where do we start?"

"Here's the sequence," I reply. "First the pastry, then the lemon filling, and finally the meringue. To start, we'll need a large bowl, pastry blender, measuring cup and spoons, pie plate, and rolling pin."

Joann dives into action—flinging open cupboards and drawers, pulling out pots, pans, and utensils. The familiar scene takes her back to memories of junior high home economics.

"I can't help thinking about Mrs. Pearson's class— although I can't remember ever making anything but baking powder biscuits." Her voice trails off.

I call her bluff. "Well, here's your lesson in making pastry." I know she will show her trump card: play helpless and announce she wasn't born with the pastry gene. I've seen the routine before and stop her short. "Okay, okay," I laugh, throwing up my arms. "Let's drop the story and get started! I'll lead the way!"

I grab an apron and tie it tight around my waist, launching into instructions with the clipped authority of an emergency room doctor—simultaneously reading the recipe and embellishing the instructions with details I know by rote from watching our mother bake in her kitchen over the years.

"For the pastry: mix two teaspoons salt, one table-spoon sugar, and one teaspoon baking powder with five cups all-purpose flour. Take one pound Tenderflake lard and cut into flour mixture with pastry blender to the consistency of small pebbles. Whisk together two table-spoons vinegar and one small egg. Combine with water to equal one cup liquid ingredients. Add to flour mixture and blend. Work pastry lightly with hands, shape into round ball, and chill briefly in the fridge.

"To make the crust: take brown butcher's paper and cover with light dusting of flour, roll out pastry, cut edges to fit the pie plate. Handle pastry carefully. Slide onto plate and into a 400-degree oven for approximately ten minutes."

With the crust safely in the oven, Joann turns thought-ful, speaking softly. "You know, Dad says the only thing he regrets is not dancing with Mom as often as she wanted when they got older. Says his knees were always sore, but he knows that was no excuse for refusing her."

My throat constricts around her words. *So simple a request and yet he says no.* The silence speaks of lingering heartache.

I remind her, "We'd better start the filling." I return to the recipe. "We'll need a saucepan, whisk, zester, and lemon squeezer." Joann springs into action and we're underway.

"For the filling: separate three eggs—yolks for the filling and whites for the meringue. Set whites aside. Combine in saucepan one cup sugar, five tablespoons cornstarch, and one-eighth teaspoon salt with two cups milk. Whisk continuously ten to twelve minutes over medium heat until mixture thickens. Add three beaten yolks, three tablespoons butter, one-third cup fresh-squeezed lemon juice, and zest. Stir gently another six to eight minutes until bubbles appear on surface and begin to pop. Remove pan from burner and wait for filling to cool. Pour filling into pastry shell and start the meringue.

"In Mixmaster bowl, whisk together three tablespoons sugar, three egg whites, one-quarter teaspoon cream of tartar, and a half teaspoon vanilla. Beat on high until whites are firm. To test consistency, turn the bowl upside down. If meringue clings to the sides without sliding out, you are ready to assemble.

"To assemble: scoop a series of large dollops of meringue from the bowl, and with a flick-of-the-wrist technique, flop meringue onto the filling and attach to edges of the crust. Spread lightly to centre and form into satin peaks."

I turn to Joann and announce the culmination of our work with a rousing declaration. "This is it. This is the best part of the process—the moment we've waited for! Here's where we stand back and admire our creation. And it's time to bake the meringue—ten to fifteen minutes."

Joann has earned the honour of placing the pie in the oven and handles it with the same care as if she were sliding fine porcelain into a kiln. She closes the oven door gently. I look through the oven window to check it myself. Straightening up, I give her a barely perceptible nod.

A startled look crosses her face. "Something weird just happened," she says. She turns her head as if she is listening. I put down the measuring cup I am washing.

"Did you feel that?" she asks. "Like a swish of air just swept into the room!"

"Yes," I say. "There's no mistaking it." We both feel a familiar energy that can only be Mom's spirit—returning after three years dead—and arriving in the nick of time to issue final instructions. Although she is no longer in physical form, our mother exhibits an impressive force of character. Not bothering with words, she communicates in a non-verbal frequency that is more felt than heard. Her transmission downloads clear and crisp.

Remember, meringue is finicky. Always turn the oven down before cooking. Too low a heat will dry it out. Too high a heat will shrink the egg whites and you'll watch with dismay as your darling meringue shrivels to half its height by the time you're ready to eat.

Pooooof! Just like that—it'll be all over.

Not that the pie won't still be delicious, but nowhere as showy without those stiff satin peaks!

Not daring to trifle with Mom's time-tested tips, we lunge for the dial and reset the oven to 340 degrees.

I lower my voice and lean toward Joann. "Maybe she's here to take him home."

"It's possible," she says.

"Well, for the time being she can join us for tea."

While Joann and I wait in the kitchen for the meringue to golden, Dad detects a different energy in the house and perks up. His voice, sure and animated, floats up from the sofa, taking on a life of its own. "You know I might be crazy, and I know she's gone, but I think your mother's here with us. Just couldn't stay away from the fun. It was always her favourite time—when you girls were together with us. Together," he repeats, "and not coming and going, one by one."

At four in the afternoon we gather around the wicker table set up on the porch with a white antique cloth and our parents' wedding china and flatware. The sun lays a dappled light over the lawn and garden; the wind settles to a murmur.

Tea time means different things to Dad, Joann, and me. I hand Dad a glass of Scotch neat, Joann a glass of prosecco, and pour myself a cup of Red Rose tea—the same blend I began drinking with Mom as a teenager.

The pie rests quietly in the centre of the table, awaiting proclamations of praise. The meringue with its proud peaks revels in its tour de force, and the whole affair is worthy of first place in the Smithers Fall Fair. We are a family once again, the four of us—feeling the delicious perfection of the day. By the time the pie is three-quarters eaten, Dad has savoured his second piece. Joann has topped up her glass, I've poured myself another cup of tea, and Mom's presence has dissipated.

TWO WEEKS AFTER my visit, Dad dies at the age of seventy-five, but it is not until years of reviewing the sofa scenes and the events that follow that I begin to distill certain meaning from our last weekend together. And while I cannot say for certain what triggers the impulse to write a story, file his nails, and ultimately bake him a pie, inherent in serving the impulse is the desire to fix things between us. To offer a connection we rarely felt.

Now, almost twenty-five years after his death, I see these gestures through a symbolic lens: the story—a reckoning of why he could not express his love directly; the nails—a filing away of the harsh edge we all felt; and the pie—an offering of sweetness and the experience of being together as a family. All of which I believe eased his passing.

Looking over our shared lives, I imagine each of us— two daughters and a father—participating in an ancient mystery and acting out the rituals of preparing the dying for an imminent death.

ALL OF WHICH is right and good.

GRATITUDE

Deepest gratitude

. . . to the writing pros who polished this book and collaborated with me.

Eva Hunter, writing coach who transformed my manuscript during an intensive stay in Greece; Kristin Masters, copy editor and fast-to-respond friend; Inge Hardman, photographer and website designer, for her warmth and gorgeous work; and my excellent literary agency Page Two, with Trena White, Gabrielle Narsted, Peter Cocking, Zoe Grams, and Jenny Govier. Together we created dynamic, honest, and deeply satisfying relationships and crafted a book that delights the senses.

Deepest gratitude

. . . to friends and family who listened to my stories and walked with me.

Victor Lindal, stalwart companion on the Camino de Santiago; Eda Lishman, fellow writer who heard the first story during a retreat in Mexico; and for their constancy, Barb Crombie, William Baker, Susan Peters, Rohanna Goodwin-Smith, Margaret Angus, Marsha Douglas, Rita Leroux, Roger Watt, Val Rutter, Joann Hetherington, Sarah Nattrass, and Brian and Mary Nattrass.

Deepest gratitude

. . . to my first readers.

Annette Aubrey, Jan DeGrass, Judith Fewster, Susan Freeman, Arden Henley, Krista MacKinnon, Cassidy Merriam, Susan Page, Sheila Peters, and P.J. Reece.

Deepest gratitude

. . . for Spirit's creative gifts, which have shaped this collection and sustained me while writing. I shall always be amazed by the beauty and genius.

ABOUT THE AUTHOR

PATRICIA HETHERINGTON's career path has encompassed teaching, training, and selling real estate for twenty years. At midlife she changed gears to complete a master's degree, becoming a counsellor and publishing the memoir *The Winter Gardener: A Woman's Journey from Futile to Fertile* (2007). She has walked unharmed on hot coals to impress a new lover and trekked the Camino de Santiago in Spain. In 2016 she quit her day job, throwing back the covers and pushing forward to publish a new book. She lives on the Sunshine Coast of British Columbia, Canada.

Visit Patricia online at: www.patriciahetherington.ca